What people are s
Wait is Not a Four-letter Word:

The book, *Wait is Not a Four-letter Word* is not just a wake-up book written to the singles; it addresses practical issues, not meant to prolong your waiting or put you indefinitely in the queue. But rather, it connects you to godly principles with an opportunity for self-examination, transitioning from waiting to the fulfillment and possession of God's will for you.

This book reveals the heartbeat of God for the singles in this drive-through generation. It points to the fact you can enjoy your waiting period and still be committed to victorious Christian living.

Dr. Rotimi Iyun graciously and extensively researched the issue of waiting from her experience and God's view. You can almost palpate her passion and wisdom as she pops out of the pages of this book.

I strongly recommend this book to every single, their parents, friends, and church family. It is a godly pill that will promote healthy relationships among the singles.

—Matilda Abiola—Senior Pastor, Christ
Life Bible Church, Brooklyn, New York

Wait is Not a Four Letter Word is a timely book not just for singles but also for the body of Christ. Many of us have created Ishmaels because we were unwilling to wait for God's perfect timing and for God's best. Rotimi Iyun has done an excellent job teaching us about how to thrive at every stage and state of our lives and not to think happiness can only come when we get married and have children. I love this quote from her book: "I have made up my mind to live life to the fullest. It shouldn't matter whether I get married or stay single, what should matter is that I fulfill my purpose." A beautiful woman who is willing to wait for the one God made for her and live each day serving and loving God. A must read book for single women, great Bible study for single adults, and a great tool for churches to help love and embrace people in their churches in every stage of their lives.

—LaNell Miller—Co-Pastor, Church
on the Rock, Texarkana

The book is vintage Rotimi who doesn't like doing things half done. It is a book that has looked at this topic from every angle imaginable so that no matter who you are, if you have been waiting, you will find yourself there. Be that as it may, I would not say it has an answer for everyone, only the Bible can fit that bill.

I say it is vintage Rotimi because in reading through, Rotimi has not hidden herself but taken the reader on her own journey as she waits. Due to its practicality, it makes it an interesting read.

I am glad a book like this is out, I am sure it will bring much blessing to the church and beyond.

Maybe this is the reason Rotimi had to wait...Have you found yours?

—Elekima Ekine—Resident Pastor, Christ Chapel
Int'l Churches, Ashi, Ibadan, Nigeria

What a title, a cheeky introduction that pokes at your curiosity to delve into this book on relationships as it affects the single for whatever reasons woman.

If the call to wait on God, His timing and will has always baffled you as a woman; this book is the key to unlock its mysteries.

A delightful easy-to-read and interesting guide full of important information for those of us who want to enjoy the single stage or state of our lives without apologies to any. The book sizzles with brave energy to deal with a subject a lot may shy away from, sex and the single woman, divorce, separation, rape, abstinence, sexual abuse, and remarriage.

The author was able to take an everyday subject and turn it into a compelling read that I enjoyed and could realistically relate to and highly recommend to all. *Wait is Not a Four-letter Word* employs eloquent and imaginative use of language, pulse-pounding truths, backed by Scriptures that keeps you turning the pages. Handling this complex subject was presented in user-friendly terms.

I recommend this riveting book.

—OYINDAMOLA SODERU—PASTOR, FOUNTAIN OF
LIFE CHURCH, ILUPEJU, LAGOS, NIGERIA

It is said that churches today sometimes fail to recognize "singleness" as a calling and in the words of Apostle Paul it is indeed a "calling"; a state to be enjoyed and not endured. A time of purposeful living and destiny shaping. *Wait is Not a Four-Letter Word* is therefore a timely book that is well written and highly inspiring.

Rotimi has provided a balance and an in depth manual for the single woman to navigate life successfully. I highly recommend the book.

—ADEFUNKE EKINE—DIRECTOR, YOUTH CARE DEVELOPMENT AND EMPOWERMENT INITIATIVE (YcDEI) AND CO-PASTOR, CHRIST CHAPEL INT'L CHURCHES, ASHI, IBADAN, NIGERIA

This is it! I like this book! This is the best book I have personally read on singlehood. It is all-embracing written with warmth, in all blatant honesty and yes, with personal experience (not a helicopter view) and life applications. All the disturbing questions, thoughts that are thrust deep inside, and fears you dare not express are all treated. It takes a lot of courage to write this kind of book in the society we are in, and I salute that courage and the push to help humanity that brought it out. I just intended to gloss over it, but the book pulled my attention and left me better after reading it. Well done once again!

—ADESOLA ADESOKAN—PASTOR, CHRIST CHAPEL INT'L CHURCHES, ASHI, IBADAN, NIGERIA

Wait

is Not a Four-Letter Word

The Mature Woman's Guide to
Living Single with Grace and Purpose

ROTIMI IYUN

Foreword by Funke Felix-Adejumo

j44 MEDIA

ISBN: 978-1-948977-00-5 (paperback)
ISBN: 978-1-948977-01-2 (ebook/epub)
ISBN: 978-1-948977-02-9 (ebook/mobi & Kindle)

Author photograph by Hannah Ojatuwase.
Book design by DesignForBooks.com

Dedication

For my mom—Adamito Oluremi Iyun,
affectionately known as Mama.

For the sacrifices you have made

For the prayers prayed

For the examples given

For the love shown

You are one is a million, Mama, and your strength
through the years has been an inspiration.

When things got tough, you would sing "Agbara Baba
Ka o, Agbara Jesu Ka" (God's power is enough to
handle this, Jesus' power is enough). You would call
on the husband to the widow and the father to the
fatherless, and He would show up every single time.

I would not be the woman I am today if not
for your example. Thank you for letting me be
myself, i.e., the much quieter version of you!

I love you, Mama!

Your special Pal

Contents

Foreword

The concept of "waiting" is one that has become alien to this generation. Everything is in the fast lane, and people want their needs met NOW! Standards, traditions, and cultural beliefs set by men and women who probably did not have an encounter with God have become the Holy Grail for how we run our lives, and these standards often influence our eventual outcome. Decisions made under such influence tend to yield little or no result.

This book opens us up to the suggested standards that the world proposes and also guides us through the accepted standards that God expects. Books like these are important to every single man and woman out there. It's a must read!

Rotimi Iyun is a woman of virtue and great grace, endowed with God's wisdom to deal with the vices of the devil for both single and married people. And through this wisdom, she has done extensive research, coupled with a vast experience in helping young ladies become women of impact and influence and also develop the right perspective to better manage the different phases of their lives.

In this book, you will find practical truths on handling challenges faced as a single person and also understanding your season and reason for being single, etc.

I pray that as you read through this book, God will open the eyes of your understanding, make you a better person, and also strengthen you to be the best version of you He has created.

—Funke Felix-Adejumo
Agape Christian Ministries, Akure, Nigeria.
President, Funke Felix
Adejumo Foundation.
Author of over fifty books such as *Fifty Lessons Life Taught Me, My Seed is Designed for the Palace*, and *Mothers Summit Prayer Points*
http://www.funkefelixadejumo.org/

Introduction

L ife for single Christian women has never been tougher than it is today. With the advent of social media, what was once considered private is now paraded before everyone for the entire world to see. Everywhere we turn, we are bombarded with images of perfect couples and the perceived stigma of being single. Single has become a synonym for being lonely, unfulfilled, unwanted, and frustrated. The voices that say otherwise are drowning in the sea of social norms and opinions.

I came to Christ at the tender age of nine and have lived as a Christian ever since making that decision almost thirty years ago. As a teenager growing up in the church, I attended every marriage seminar I could and prayed about my future husband. I had the perfect plan—two Masters or a Ph.D. by twenty-five, followed by marriage, two kids before thirty, after which I would start my consulting practice.

It has been said, if you want to see if God has a sense of humor, just tell Him all the plans you have for your life. I got my first Masters, but it came at thirty followed by the doctorate in Theology at thirty-three. I am still waiting for the rest of my plans to come to fruition.

I find myself surrounded by many other wonderful women navigating this life who are not married as they had imagined, but single. As the years have passed and I have moved from my 20s to early 30s and into the late 30s, I have experienced firsthand the changes in support systems and available resources for single women as they get older.

Unfortunately, most churches do not seem to know what to do with older, single women as we do not fit neatly into traditional niches. I found that attending the singles fellowship automatically makes me a facilitator as there are young women in their early twenties who are not bothered with the issues that concern me at this age. The women's fellowship has more women my age, but the conversations tend to run more along the lines of how to keep a marriage and raise kids. I see the same challenges for divorced women, widows, and single parents, who all struggle to find a place where they can connect and talk through issues peculiar to this time of their life.

I wondered why certain subjects rarely seem to be addressed—like how to handle the loneliness often associated with singleness, the hopefully "unsatisfied" sexual desires in an increasingly sexual world, the longing for children, and fears about living alone. Who do you talk to about the slights, perceived or actual because you are single? Who can you talk to after another encounter with your ex or even worse, your ex's new wife?

Current statistics show the number of singles "Never Married," "Divorced," and "Widowed" are at an all-time high and show no signs of abating.

I wrote this book to try to bridge that gap and help other women navigate this period with grace. In meeting and talking to other single women, they consistently tell me they are encouraged by my attitude as a single woman and my decision to enjoy this period in my life. I struggled for many years over writing this book as I wondered if this attitude was preventing me from getting married. As I prayed over this book, I have been encouraged to go ahead and share some things I have learned along the way—trusting that God will translate these words into what you need to hear for your unique situation. This book is not intended to teach you how to date or court—it is intended to help you be the best you can be while you are still single.

One of the most vital lessons I have learned is that "Wait is not a four-letter word." You are probably well aware that most euphemisms or swear words are four-letter words. As Christians, we have learned to avoid saying these words and keep our speech clean to accurately reflect Christ. In the same manner, we have come to the point in society and the church where we want everything done instantly. Waiting is a word that seems to have gone out of fashion in our microwave world where everything seems to come with a snap of the fingers. We want miracles that happen immediately rather than endure the lengthy process of trusting God to achieve the same results.

As single women looking forward to the joy of marriage, it is easy to succumb to the pressures of the world and rush ahead of the will of God for our lives. In spite of the prevailing sentiment, it is important to discern the difference between a delay and a proper time of waiting by seeking God's face to appropriately handle the period of waiting.

Waiting occurs at various levels. Waiting to go into a relationship, waiting to have sex within the sanctity of marriage, and even waiting to get married. However, society provides various excuses for why singles should rush in these areas; parental pressure, peer pressure, sexual pressure, and ultimately fear. In light of statements like, "Your biological clock is ticking," and "Everyone is doing it," singles need solid reasons to consider waiting.

Unfortunately, waiting has become synonymous with a holding pattern where we just hang on to life until we are lucky enough to snatch or be snatched up by an eligible man. Many women hold back on life for fear that living life to the full as a single woman will repel or handicap their chances at marriage.

I will attempt to examine the reasons we are still single and if this is something that can be remedied. We will spend time talking about remarriage—for the divorced or widowed, as well as for a single mother. I will also discuss expectations about what marriage will bring, how to deal with our sexuality, and how to develop the right attitude while waiting. We will walk through the proper definition of waiting and how to live life to the fullest during this period of singleness. I will then close with a letter written on your behalf to your family, church, and friends that you can hopefully share to help them deal with you in wisdom.

There are questions and applications at the end of each chapter designed to help you apply the truths presented honestly and practically. But this only works if you answer these questions honestly and follow through on any changes required to practice any new behavior.

I got a Fitbit some time ago to encourage myself to walk a lot more. One day, my nephew offered to wear it to help me hit my 10,000 step goal for the day—a practice I have seen amongst many people engaged in a competition. The truth of the matter is, I can deceive people about how many steps I have taken and how healthy I am; but I cannot deceive myself when I take shortcuts on a regimen designed to bring personal benefit to my life. I want to encourage you not to cut any corners. Be brutally honest with yourself and take definite steps to make this "wait" journey a worthwhile experience for yourself!

I pray this book blesses you and gives you practical steps you can take going forward. God made you special, and I want you to know I am walking this walk with you and we will do this with grace!

Wait—Whose Fault Is it Anyway?

I remember sitting in a meeting in my early twenties where the preacher delved into the growing trend of older women in the church who were unmarried. His conviction was that a lot of these women had missed their season of marriage—that period when they received a lot of offers and didn't choose.

I wondered if an abundance of offers necessarily translated to good choices. Over the course of the past several years, I have pondered this question as I watched various friends, acquaintances, and maybe even enemies tie the knot. I have gone through the early arrogant days of thinking the right man was just around the corner and waiting for me, to the despair of wondering if marriage would ever happen to me. I applied my analytical mind to find what I might be doing wrong that is contributing to this delay. Why do I have to wait and not Susan down the street? Why does she get the opportunity to get married at twenty-five and start a family while I still have to wait? Am I not praying enough? Am I praying incorrectly? Am I saying no to the

> *Am I single for a reason or single for a season?*

eligible men God is sending my way? Am I waiting for God to bring someone to me instead of going out to mix with eligible singles my age? Am I single for a reason or single for a season?

WHY ARE YOU NOT MARRIED?

I have not yet been able to find a suitable response to the often insensitive question, "You love the Lord, you're beautiful, have a good job, the total package so, why are you not married?" I have toyed with different answers in my mind—"No one answered the 'husband wanted' ad," "There are no good men left," "Are you interviewing for the position?" "I don't know, when you find out will you let me know?" I always ask myself how many people would walk up to a childless couple and ask, "Why don't you have any children?"

Human nature wants life to be tied up in a pretty bow and for everything to have a rational explanation. Thus, the marriage question is a prelude to trying to find a reason to either placate or explain away the "delay" in attaining marital bliss.

WHY OTHER PEOPLE THINK WE ARE NOT MARRIED

People have different opinions when it comes to singleness, and most feel free to express their opinions whether you want to listen to them or not.

Let me share some perspectives I have been offered over the years to see if any of these strike a chord with you:

- **When God comes late, He comes big.** My standard response to that is, "Did He come small for you because you got married early?" Does the fact that I am marrying later in life guarantee my child will be a John the Baptist? The evidence around me doesn't quite support the claim that delay means my family will be greater than yours. We see our friends who marry late and guess what—they have to work on their marriages just as hard as those who married earlier.

- **If you had been married, you might have been divorced or childless by now.** God might have been preventing you from sadness and loss, so He is asking you to wait instead. I think this oversimplifies the complexity of divorce, as it assumes it is totally dependent on one person's behavior. However, I have seen people transformed as God worked on them to refine some obvious character flaws that seemed to give them a better chance at a lasting marriage.

- **You are not ready.** I wonder why it would take so long to prepare me for marriage. Am I really so messed up that I am still under construction, ten, twenty years after my age-mates have gotten married!

- **Your expectations are too high; you need to lower your standards.** I always wonder if the

person who says this would repeat it in front of
their spouse as an admission they lowered their
standards in making their choice. But alas, I am not
in the business of breaking up homes, so I have yet
to see how that one would play out.

❧ **God is working on your future husband.** This
is fine, but I wish God would hurry up or give me
someone who takes less time to put together.

WHY WE THINK WE ARE NOT MARRIED

As if we don't get enough flak from people, we have our
own opinions on the matter.

❧ **The right person hasn't turned up yet**. This is
the default response, as one would hope that if the
right person had already turned up, we would be
married.

❧ **It just hasn't worked out yet.** This removes the
focus from the other person to the relationship stars
not aligning. This could be due to either of you not
being ready for commitment at the time, issues that
may or may not have been resolvable, poor timing,
or other significant events trumping the relationship,
or even external factors like parental dissent.

❧ **I don't deserve to be married.** You may have some
pain or event in your past that makes you think you
do not deserve to be married. It doesn't matter what
you have done in the past, you are a new creature

in Christ and entitled to all the blessings of God. All of us have freely received everything we have as a gift from God. You are just as entitled to the gift of marriage as the Virgin Mary was because of the sacrifice of Jesus Christ.

> **I messed up the first time.** Society is not always kind to divorcees or widows who would like to remarry. Some congregations will not allow remarriage after a divorce based on their interpretation of Scripture. We will deal with this topic in greater detail in a later chapter. Suffice it to say that God is a God of second chances and He has the best in store for you.

WHAT IF GOD IS TO BLAME?

Maybe your position is the reason you are not married is not because of something you haven't done. I was saved from a young age and have spent all my life in church. I had been taught that if I serve God with all my heart, He will bring the right man my way. However, as I got older, I saw other women who didn't serve God with the same reckless abandon, who have no issues going in and out of relationships, and who for all intents and purposes, settle down into happy homes. This is a common sentiment among "good girls," because we believe we are entitled to the best men in the church because we were privileged to know God at an early age.

I heard a preacher say once that even if God does nothing else after saving us, He has already done more than

God does not respond to what we do; we respond to what God does

enough. So yes, I have had to adjust my attitude to acknowledge I do not deserve it; instead, I will receive it as a gift from God. The thing about gifts is they are freely given and often undeserved. I had to learn to shift the focus off what I do to what God does! It's just like the Jews and their claim to God. Salvation was from the Jews, but in the end, salvation was a gift from God.

So where does that leave our proud Jewish insider claims and counterclaims? Canceled. Yes, canceled. What we've learned is this: God does not respond to what we do; we respond to what God does. We've finally figured it out. Our lives get in step with God and everyone else by letting Him set the pace, not by proudly or anxiously trying to run the parade.

But by shifting our focus from what we do to what God does, don't we cancel out all our careful keeping the rules and ways God commanded? Not at all. What happens is that by putting that entire way of life in its proper place, we confirm it (Romans 3:27–28, 31 MSG).

I have always found the book of Job interesting because it gives me comfort when I go through challenges. Job reminds me that I am human, and just sifting through his responses, we can see a range of emotions through his ordeal:

> ❧ It's too late for me; I should never have been born (Job 3, 6:11).

- God is choosing not to answer me (Job 6:8 MSG).

- God is picking on me (Job 7:19–21).

- God is Almighty—He does what He pleases (Job 9:32–34).

- God is waiting for me to mess up (Job 10:13–17).

- God is mad at me (Job 13:20–27).

- There is no special reward for serving God (Job 21:7–15).

- God is not just (Job 27:1–4).

- God has forsaken me (Job 29:1–5).

- I have been righteous and don't deserve this (Job 31).

God's response to Job's pain can be summarized in Job 40:8, *"Would you discredit my justice? Would you condemn me to justify yourself?"*

I learned from God's response to Job that I cannot see or understand everything that happens to me in this life.

I need to trust God's justice when I can't understand what is going on around me.

I need to believe God is a rewarder of those who diligently seek Him and He is doing the best for me.

I need to trust in God's goodness and omnipotence, even when I cannot figure out a logical reason for why things are not happening the way I want them to.

So no, I can't tell you why you are still not married, but I can turn you to the One who can do something about it.

SINGLE FOR A REASON

The natural preponderance of opinion is we are single for a reason and not for a season. It would be naïve to assume we are all finished works simply waiting for the right man to come along—most of us are a work in progress. We are all single for a reason, and most of us are single for a season. One does not negate the other. What is important is that while in the season of singleness, we are actively working on removing the reasons for singleness.

This Is My Choice

I do not like eggplants aka garden eggs! Fry it, cook it, bake it, put it in lasagna, or season it, I have not yet met an eggplant dish I enjoy. Whenever I am offered an eggplant dish, I respectfully decline, explaining it is not to my taste. I cannot count the number of "chefs" who assure me that my aversion would be abolished once I tasted their concoction. Hence, I have times when I cannot get out of it gracefully. The truth is, I am comfortable with never tasting eggplant until I go to be with Jesus. I am not trying out the rare eggplant dish because I need to prove it is edible. I am perfectly content to watch other people enjoying the eggplant dishes. I am only trying it to please the person who offered it to me.

In a similar vein, I have come to the personal realization that some women sincerely do not want to be married and have an extremely hard time convincing people this is what they truly want. What makes it harder is the number of women who vowed not to get married only to change their minds when they met "the man." We will go into more detail about the decision to stay single later in this book. Suffice to say, as long as your decision is sound, you do not need to be bullied out of that position by family and friends.

What am I doing wrong?

I write this section with a considerable amount of trepidation because I think we as mature single women already receive enough bashing from other sources. However, it would be remiss of me to avoid pointing out some issues we need to deal with as women. Conveniently, it is easier to see these reasons in other women rather than in ourselves. Another complication is that what we typically identify in ourselves as valid reasons are things we recognize as flaws in other married women. Let me give some examples—Some of the most quarrelsome women I have met are married (I don't know if I can say happily married). Growing up, we were told cooking was the way to a man's heart. I am sure you know a great cook who is not married or is currently having issues in her home. All models are not married, and not all obese women are single. We will not always be able to find a reason to explain why things happen the way they do. Like the story in the gospels about the man blind from birth, the reason for being unmarried may be something totally unexpected.

> "As Jesus was passing by, He saw a man blind from birth. His disciples asked Him, 'Rabbi, who sinned, this man or his parents, that he was born blind?' Jesus answered, 'Neither this man nor his parents sinned,

but this happened that the works of God would be displayed in him'" (John 9:1–3).

This is not to downplay the importance of growing in God and working through obvious character flaws. Your future husband should not be on the shortlist for sainthood just because he was brave enough to date you despite your quirks. We have a responsibility to be women of virtue, and we need to learn how to make this a lifelong pursuit.

In this pursuit, we would do well to help each other become better women as well.

IRON SHARPENS IRON

"As iron sharpens iron, so one person sharpens another" (Proverbs 27:17).

This is a responsibility I take pretty seriously. I had a dear friend and roommate who I discovered tended to be irritable when touched. I made it my duty to touch her hand or tap her shoulder at regular intervals. She would snap and say, "Don't touch me—talk to me if you need to get my attention." I would patiently wait for about one minute and repeat the action (yes, I was the youngest child in my family). At the height of her frustration, I would calmly inform her—"I have been sent to teach you patience. Are you going to snap at your husband and children whenever they touch you?"

As time progressed, she stopped snapping and calmly turned when tapped on the shoulder. At this time, my work was done, and I let her be. I don't mean to imply the help in growth was one-sided. I learned to go to sleep with the light on, deal with having the TV on rather than radio silence, to bridle my tongue, and speak the truth in love. This was crucial because I was a grown woman and used to doing things my way. After she got married, she told me I would not believe how alike her husband and I turned out to be in certain respects. I like to think we rubbed off on each other and became much better women for it. This also worked because it was intentional and not contentious. Our motive must stem from love and a desire to help other women become the best version of themselves they can be.

SINGLE FOR A SEASON

What if it is no one's fault that you are single? Is it possible this is simply a question of times and seasons? I know if I choose to live on an archaeological dig in the middle of nowhere for years on end, or work on the moon, my chances of getting married are pretty slim. In situations like this, it is perfectly possible to do everything right and still see a "delay" in getting married. One of my all-time favorite Scriptures is David's cry to God when he was facing one of his numerous battles, *"My times are in your hands"* (Psalm 31:15a).

My seasons, my days, my triumphs, my losses, my ups, and my downs; my times are in Your hands, God. In the end, the all-encompassing factor is not how I position myself or set myself up. We cannot take out the involvement and intervention of God in our lives. The writer of Ecclesiastes put it beautifully: *"He has made everything beautiful in its time. He has also set eternity in the human heart; yet no one can fathom what God has done from beginning to end"* (Ecclesiastes 3:11).

Accepting that God is involved in the seasons of my life is not the sticking point; the problem is God doesn't see time the way I see it.

> *"But do not forget this one thing, dear friends: With the Lord a day is like a thousand years, and a thousand years are like a day"* (2 Peter 3:8).

There is an old joke I read in *Reader's Digest* many years ago that I think perfectly captures the dilemma we face with trusting that God has our seasons in hand.

> *A man was speaking to God, and asked Him, "God is it true that to you a thousand years is a minute?"*
>
> *"That's true," God replied.*
>
> *"And is it true that to you $1,000,000 is like a penny?"*
>
> *"That's true," God said.*
>
> *"Well, you see I was wondering if you could give me a penny," asked the man.*
>
> *"Sure," said God, "just wait a minute."*

While I have always found this joke extremely funny, I can relate to the fear that comes with understanding the difference in how God perceives time. I find myself telling God—if You really wait 1,000 years to give me a husband, I would be dead by then.

WHAT TIME IS IT?

I found some interesting characteristics of time that I would love to share with you.

- **Time is different for everyone.** Looking at the world itself, we see time is different all over the world. There is even a line where it is a different day on either side. In the same manner, people will wait different lengths of time to get married, and this is not explainable by simple science. Just as we do not leave the earth in the same order we came into it; we need to accept our times are not the same. Who are you to say you have been delayed when you don't even know what time it is for you?

- **Time is dependent on where you are.** Your location has a bearing on your timing. Sometimes your period of waiting is tied to where you are in life's journey—spiritually, materially, physically, etc. If you travel west over the Pacific late in the day, you will cross the international date line and lose a day. It is possible to leave on a Wednesday and arrive on a Friday with Thursday not existing for you. The same is true in reverse where you can live the same day twice.

- **Time is dependent on what you do.** Imagine two people driving down a stretch of road. One drives down to the end of the road to reach her home and is in no particular hurry. The other stands to win some money, depending on how fast she can

get to the end of the road. In one case, the focus
is on finishing the race while the other focuses
more on the time it takes to finish the race. When
time becomes the most important factor in an
event, it becomes a competition to see who snags
the husband first, etc. Paul reminds us that those
comparing themselves to themselves are not wise!
(2 Corinthians 10:12)

- **Time is dependent on what you see.** Our concept
of time is finite and different, i.e., we cannot see
what God sees. We view time in the context of
quantifiable periods, e.g., days and hours, which
is aka Chronos, from where we get the word
chronology. God sees time in seasons, e.g., the time
to bless you is now [Kairos]. This fundamental
difference creates significant tension as we count out
days and hours while God is looking at the overall
purpose He has planned for us. I imagine Elizabeth
crying to God, "My biological clock is ticking," and
God responding, "I do not need your biological
clock to give you children. You see Elizabeth, your
son, John, needs to come just before my Son Jesus
will come on earth because he is a forerunner. He
will point people to Jesus. I have chosen Mary
to carry Him to the earth, but she was just born
yesterday, so we need to wait for the days and hours
to pass until she is old enough to carry a child. I
have promised you a child. Will you trust that I will
bring My word to pass over you?"

IN CONCLUSION

> *"I have seen something else under the sun:*
> *The race is not to the swift or the battle to the*
> *strong, nor does food come to the wise or wealth to the*
> *brilliant or favor to the learned; but time and chance*
> *happen to them all"* (Ecclesiastes 9:11).

I firmly believe God's arm is not short. God is able to give me a husband today. I also believe God will continue to work to make me the woman He has called me to be. He is a loving father and is always working out the best for me. I have settled in my mind that since I am not married now, it's not material to fulfilling God's plan for me right now. I refuse to live life looking for someone or something to blame for my being single. What I can control is my behavior while I am single. I have made it my goal to learn to be content, for if I am not content as a single woman, I will not be content in marriage.

What I can control is my behavior while I am single.

> *"Nevertheless, each person should live as a believer in*
> *whatever situation the Lord has assigned to them, just*
> *as God has called them. This is the rule I lay down in*
> *all the churches"* (1Corinthians 7:17).

I chose to make this time of singlehood a time of ministry, growth, and blessing. I hear God say, "Wait for My best, child, and you will not be disappointed." I chose to wait because "Wait is not a four-letter word."

LIFE APPLICATION

1. Write down the first five words that come to your mind as synonyms for single (This only works if you do it honestly).

    Do you have mostly positive or negative words on your list?

    Think through why these words made it on your list. Are they true representations of the single state?

    For each word, identify one of the following actions.

    Reinforce positive words

    Replace negative words

2. Have you ever been asked, "Why are you not married?"

    How does this question make you feel? Angry, sad, indifferent?

    Develop a graceful response to the question, "Why are you not married?"

3. Over the next week, ask God to show you anything that may be preventing you from getting into or staying in a relationship that would lead to marriage.

4. Reach out to people close to you who will give you honest feedback. Ask if there are any traits or concerns they feel you need to work on.

   Develop an action plan to deal with each reason you have identified.

Wait—I Already Had My Chance

MONOPOLY

One chance! In the hustle and bustle of my hometown in Lagos, Nigeria, some years ago, this was a phrase bus conductors shouted giving you the opportunity to pick the last space on a bus. This was a prime spot, as it meant you didn't have to wait any longer. Because of this, people would jostle to pick up that last slot. Over time, this became a trap to lure unsuspecting passengers into a bus, rob them, and let them off at a deserted location. What had once meant speed, now meant danger.

Sadly, in so many cases, relationships today have become like this. Sometimes you are oblivious to the danger or are in such a hurry to change your name you cease to be aware of your surroundings. It doesn't matter what the reason is; the result is you have been robbed and let off at a deserted location of divorce.

Maybe you were married, and it didn't work out. You might have gotten your "one chance" in a relationship. You got married to that great or not so great guy. When things got tough, you tried to work through your issues, but unfortunately you ended up being divorced. You may have walked out yourself because of abuse or simply not knowing better. Whatever route you took, you ended up divorced and now wonder if you have blown the only chance you had.

Or you were in a great relationship and messed it up. Maybe it wasn't really your fault. You did everything right and still ended up on the curb with your relationship. Your dreams of happily ever after are broken, and you are one of the statistics you tried so hard to avoid.

You may not have gotten married but ended up with a child by mutual consent or rape.

Maybe your story is you had a great relationship and sadly became widowed at an early age.

Sometimes the scars you carry prevent you from moving past the self-imposed prison of pain from your past.

Unfortunately, there is no crystal ball to predict which relationships will stand the test of time or end prematurely with death or sickness.

It's like the game of Monopoly—no amount of skill can guarantee you will never pick up the dreaded *"Go to Jail"* card. Who doesn't hate to read those words, "Go Directly to Jail, Do not pass Go, Do not collect $200!"? Failed relationships are similar. You watch other people make progress and advance in other areas while it seems you are stuck in jail. Eventually, you get out, but sometimes the scars you carry prevent you from moving past the self-imposed prison of pain from your past.

The simple truth is, the challenges facing a divorcee, single mother, or widow are somewhat different from those of a single woman without any apparent baggage. You may find yourself in the awkward position where you don't fully fit in with the married women's fellowship or the singles fellowship in your local assembly. You are essentially stuck between both worlds.

SO YOU WENT THROUGH A DIVORCE

The position of most divorced women is often untenable as it seems you can't win for losing. If you successfully get over the pain and stick your toe in the water, you have to deal with the church's differing philosophies on whether divorced women should remarry or whether remarriage constitutes adultery. If you can overcome that hurdle, you may face resentment from other singles because you are now competing with them for the few eligible men, and they believe you have more "experience" in this area. Add children to the mix and things can quickly spiral out of control.

One thing I have always struggled with is the various church stances on the subject of divorce and remarriage. With the passage of time, the number of divorces within the church has greatly increased, and in most cases, we do not have a cohesive stance on remarriage. In some instances, there is almost a "don't ask, don't tell" approach to avoid taking a stance.

Simmering under the surface are many questions we struggle to find answers to.

- How do we reconcile the concept of a loving and forgiving God with a God who condemns a woman who obtained a divorce for any reason to a life of celibacy?
- What do we do if the divorce has already occurred—no matter how frivolous we judge the reason to be?
- Are the rules different if one or both participants was not a Christian at the time of the divorce?
- What happens if there is no hope of reconciliation, i.e., someone has remarried or will not consider coming back together?
- My husband is cheating on me, but my church doesn't believe in divorce. What are my options?
- Should I marry someone who has gone through a divorce? Will I live in sin forever or does God forgive at some point?

While I was working on my doctoral thesis[1], I recall coming to a crossroads on my views on divorce and remarriage. Here I was studying different points of view on the subject and finally having to take a stand on a topic that has bothered me for years. I remember pacing among the shelves in the library in Queens and eventually, calling my supervisor to talk through the conclusions I was coming to. Fast forward to my thesis defense, and this was the topic the examiners had the most questions about. Someone

---

1 *The Ancient Institution of Marriage and its Decline/Evolution in Modern Times* – June 2013. Christ Life Bible Institute And Seminary– An Affiliate of Lightouse Christian College and Seminary

asked me then if divorce is the worst thing that can happen to a couple and my answer was no. I may not have the facts to prove it, but I believe a lot of severely disturbed people are the products of dysfunctional marriages.

I cannot forget one of the examiners holding my hands and saying to me—"Promise me you won't stop writing." This person was married to someone who had gone through a divorce based on adultery. In spite of the "allowed" reason, there was a lingering fear of "What if I have sinned by marrying someone who was divorced?" Can you imagine the amount of pain, condemnation, and bondage that divorce has brought and continues to bring in the lives of people touched by it? I confess I do not have much personal knowledge of how devastating a divorce can be. I can only speak as an observer of human nature and share a little bit of what I have learned along the way.

I will start by saying I will always fight for the sanctity of marriage. I believe there is no marriage that cannot be saved if both parties are committed to making the relationship work. I will even go so far as to say that most troubled marriages can be saved if one party fights for that relationship to succeed. However, I have lived long enough to see women stay in physically abusive relationships or accommodate serial adultery because they have been taught they should never divorce.

As I have matured as a Christian, I have learned to separate man's doctrines or legalism from the dictates of God. I have taken time to study what God really says on this subject. I wish I could say this was totally altruistic of me, but some of this was motivated by the fact that at this age, a lot of prospective husbands are also divorced. I do not intend to deal extensively with the theology behind divorce. Instead, I encourage each woman to read the various points of view, study the Scriptures, pray about it, and then draw your conclusions. Various books deal with the subject of divorce and remarriage for each school of thought. I will address some common views on divorce, hoping to pique your interest enough to become further educated on the subject.[2]

Moses dealt extensively with divorce and remarriage in the Old Testament, providing a series of laws and considerations to take into account for when a divorce and subsequent remarriage could be undertaken. These laws were primarily to protect the woman, as the man was allowed to marry more than one woman. Moses provided a system that would free a woman to remarry, as well as empower her to petition the courts for a divorce if she was abused or maltreated. These laws were to be employed as a last resort, a fact that rapidly became lost in the application in Jewish culture. At the time of Jesus' ministry on earth, there were two prevailing camps on divorce amongst the Jews. One camp believed a woman could only be put away for adultery, while the other believed the husband could put away his wife for anything he considered an indecency. This could be something as frivolous as how she looked or dressed. Against this background, the Pharisees came to Jesus, asking which side He would weigh in on. The church's dilemma arises from reconciling Jesus' responses below and to a lesser extent—Paul's statements on this subject.

---

2 Divorce and Re-Marriage: Recovering the Biblical View by William Luck. https://bible.org/series/divorce-and-re-marriage-recovering-biblical-view

Some Pharisees came to him to test him. They asked,
"Is it lawful for a man to divorce his wife for any and
every reason?" "Haven't you read," he replied, "that
at the beginning the Creator 'made them male and
female,' and said, 'For this reason a man will leave his
father and mother and be united to his wife, and the
two will become one flesh'? So they are no longer two,
but one flesh. Therefore what God has joined together,
let no one separate." "Why then," they asked, "did
Moses command that a man give his wife a certificate
of divorce and send her away?" Jesus replied, "Moses
permitted you to divorce your wives because your
hearts were hard. But it was not this way from the
beginning. I tell you that anyone who divorces his wife,
except for sexual immorality, and marries another
woman commits adultery." (Matthew 19:3–9)[3]

There are three major schools of thought on divorce
and remarriage. The first is divorce and remarriage are
always sinful. This is due to the belief that marriage is a
permanent indissoluble union that cannot be broken under
any circumstances.

Another view is divorce is allowed under two exceptions, but remarriage is always sinful. These two exceptions
are adultery and willful desertion by an unbelieving spouse.

Finally, the last view is divorce is allowed under some
exceptions, and when these conditions are met, remarriage
is allowed.

---

3 See also Mark 10:2–12, Matthew 5:27–31

Viewpoint *1*: Divorce and Remarriage Is always Sinful

In many of the more traditional Christian circles, this is the most common view. What this means in practical terms is the divorced person is not really "single" or available, but must remain celibate for the rest of their natural life. This is expected even if they divorced when they were in their 20s and had no say in the matter, due to no-fault laws. This hardline stance is based on the premise that marriage is an indissoluble union—based on Jesus' statement "they are no longer two, but one flesh. Therefore what God has joined together, let no one separate." (Mark 10:9)

To get around this rule, many Christians in bad marriages have separated from their spouses while remaining legally married. All this does, however, is maintain the letter of the law. In other instances, people can obtain an annulment if they can prove the marriage has not been consummated. As you can imagine, two people who are desperate to get out of a marriage would gladly claim they have never had sex as long as there are no children to prove them wrong.

I do not believe this is an accurate stance since we know Jesus allowed for divorce in at least one circumstance, i.e., adultery. This leads us to the next viewpoint which states divorce is allowed under two exceptions, but remarriage is always sinful.

Viewpoint *2*: Divorce Is Allowed under Two Exceptions, but Remarriage Is Always Sinful

This viewpoint allows divorce under two notable exceptions—adultery or at the request of an unbelieving spouse.

First, let's talk about divorce being acceptable for adultery but not remarriage. From reading the words of Jesus, He seems to be saying the following:

- Divorce, except in cases of adultery, is adultery

- Whoever marries the divorced woman commits adultery

- The divorced woman who remarries commits adultery

This stance has always bothered me because my analytical mind craves answers to certain questions.

- What is responsible for breaking the marriage covenant, the adultery or the divorce? We know divorce is not mandatory after adultery. Many couples had cases where one partner committed adultery, and the aggrieved party was able to forgive, move past it, and maintain their home. If adultery can be forgiven in some instances, it cannot be the sole reason divorce is acceptable.

    Do not get me wrong—adultery (especially serial adultery) should never be tolerated. It needs to be addressed appropriately and a course of action defined. However, if we say adultery breaks the marriage covenant, we are stating there are many "married" couples today living in a broken marriage covenant.

    Our other option is to say the divorce breaks the marriage covenant. If this is true, why does a divorce work when it is adultery and not anything else?

&. What is the definition of adultery? From studying the Bible, I have learned that Jesus equates lust to adultery[4]. If my husband looks at another woman lustfully, can I claim sufficient grounds for a divorce?

&. Why does the spouse who is cheated on share the same punishment as the spouse who cheated? God made a promise to Jeremiah, stating that each person would bear the consequences of their actions. To insist that the wronged spouse be forced to remain single violates this principle.

> *"In those days people will no longer say, 'The parents have eaten sour grapes, and the children's teeth are set on edge.' Instead, everyone will die for their own sin; whoever eats sour grapes—their own teeth will be set on edge"* (Jeremiah 31:29–30).

&. Does this mean a person who was divorced and has remarried would now be committing adultery for the rest of his/her life? If remarrying is a sin, what does one now need to do to be forgiven? If I have caused a divorce by my actions, how do I make things right?

The ultimate question in my mind is this: Why does the divorcee not get a second chance?

From studying the teachings and history in the days of Jesus, I believe Jesus was addressing the penchant of the Jews of divorcing their wives for frivolous reasons.

---

4 Matthew 5:28

Jewish men were trading in their faithful wives for a newer model or divorcing their spouses purposely to be able to marry someone else without "committing adultery". I also believe if Jesus was asked to provide a complete teaching on divorce, it would be a lot longer than the few verses we currently have.

There is an Old Testament story about the daughters of Zelophedad[5] that I find fascinating. Here, we have five daughters who went up to Moses to challenge the law that only sons would receive an inheritance from their father. Moses went to God and was told to allow them to inherit their father's possessions. Further on in life, the elders of their tribe were concerned the daughters of Zelophedad would marry outside their tribe and the inheritance would be transferred to another tribe. Moses went to God again, and God told the daughters of Zelophedad that they could only marry from within the tribe of Manasseh.

> *God will reveal His principles and teach us the practical application of what His Word says.*

These women could have stayed at the first level of revelation, i.e., only sons can inherit. They did not accept this law at face value but kept going back to God to check the application of the law.

I am convinced God will reveal His principles and continue to teach us the practical application of what His Word says. We see this pattern at work with Paul who had to deal with marriages that were being broken up because one person had decided to follow Christ. Paul did not respond to this with—Jesus says you can only divorce for adultery. Paul

5 Numbers 27, 36

went to God and came back with a practical application—
if the unbelieving spouse is no longer interested in the
marriage, go ahead and grant the divorce[6]. Paul's direction
was clear—the brother or the sister is not bound in such
circumstances. The fact the brother or sister is not bound
is an indication that he or she is free of that marriage and
therefore able to remarry. I do not believe any other inter-
pretation makes sense.

Viewpoint **3**: Divorce Is Allowed under some Exceptions and Remarriage Is Allowed under Those Circumstances.

So what happens if the issue is not adultery or a lack of
faith? Are these the only reasons tenable for divorce or
remarriage? Is it then okay to file for a divorce whenever we
feel this is the only option left to us? How do we interpret
the Scripture in Malachi 2:16—God hates divorce (the act,
not the victims)?

The message in Scripture is unequivocal—marriage was
intended to last until the death of a spouse, just as it was
instituted in the beginning. Our default position, therefore,
is to guard the sanctity of marriage, along with our friends
and family, to preserve this union as God intended.[7]

If Paul or Moses were alive today, they would have a
lot to say about the particular issues we face in our time.

---

6   1 Corinthians 7:10–16

7   See Ezra 10:16–17. During the time of Ezra, there was a command
for mass divorces because the Israelites had married foreign women
who were leading their spouses astray from worshipping God. Even
though these marriages were blatantly against God's commands, there
was still a mandate to individually review each case before a divorce.

Some of these issues would be familiar. For instance, if we take a page from the days of Moses, we will find there were certain rights the woman expected from her husband. One of these was a right to fidelity. Other rights the woman had were provision and protection from abuse. If her husband did not meet those needs, she was free to seek a divorce. Divorce was not mandatory—it was a decision that one or both of the parties came to.

The wave of divorces in the church makes us wonder how many of these relationships could have been saved if things were handled differently. Be that as it may, in this sinful world, we will come across instances where legitimate reasons exist for couples to separate.[8] Spouses (yes even Christian ones) have been physically or emotionally abusive. Many marriages do not survive the loss of a child. Instances of cruelty to children, infertility, sickness, and financial mismanagement are just a few things that have driven marriages to the brink. Applying a one size fits all to every situation would be naïve, considering human nature and our varying levels of maturity.

------

8 Matthew 18:15–20

"If your brother sins against you, go and show him his fault, just between the two of you. If he listens to you, you have won your brother over. But if he will not listen, take one or two others along, so that 'every matter may be established by the testimony of two or three witnesses.' If he refuses to listen to them, tell it to the church; and if he refuses to listen even to the church, treat him as you would a pagan or a tax collector. "I tell you the truth, whatever you bind on earth will be bound in heaven, and whatever you loose on earth will be loosed in heaven.

"Again, I tell you that if two of you on earth agree about anything you ask for, it will be done for you by my Father in heaven. For where two or three come together in my name, there am I with them."

So where does this leave us? If you are divorced, whether it's your fault or not, examine yourself to ensure you can stand faultless before God on this issue. If you need to repent, God's arms are always open. As much as lies within you, make restitution for your part in the divorce. This may mean reconciliation where possible, or simply apologizing for violating the marriage covenant.

You may have chosen to stay single and have faith you will be reconciled to your ex-husband. Do this with the knowledge that reconciliation is a choice and God will not violate free will. He (your ex) is free to remarry whoever he wants to and not bound to reconcile with you. If you have decided to close that chapter of your life and move on toward a new relationship, leave your guilt and sense of failure at the feet of Jesus.

If you want to marry someone who is divorced, please make sure you are at peace with the decision and seek godly counsel. I am encouraged by the story of Joyce Meyer who went through a divorce but has been married to her second husband for over fifty years. Divorce comes with its own set of challenges, but these are by no means insurmountable. For some of us, remarriage after a divorce is not an issue in the least. For others, it is a major issue that needs to be thought through. In fact, a dear lady told me how she could not share openly that her husband had gone through a divorce in the past. I wonder how many of us remain single because we refuse to consider someone who has been divorced as eligible for marriage.

I want to appeal to every one of us to show the love of God to anyone who has gone through the pain of divorce. Don't kill the wounded soldier around you. Don't look down on someone or deem them a failure because their marriage failed! Some marriages that I have thought were solid as a rock have failed while others I had written off have weathered the storm. I have learned to say in the words of John Bradford—There but for the grace of God go I!

Let me introduce you to the miracle of grace!

The Miracle of Grace

Human nature says, you already had your chance. You made your bed, now lie in it. Why should you get a second chance with the already thin pool of men available, while others who haven't even gotten that far are still waiting?

I have good news for you—God is not like man. He is not done with you yet. He won't throw His hands up in the air and give up on you. He is a God of second chances because He always wipes the slate clean.

> *God is not like man. He is not done with you yet.*

This is the miracle of grace! It's undeserved, which means even when we don't deserve a second chance, our gracious God gives it to us!

The miracle of grace—undeserved favor is something I struggle with. Because if I want to receive grace, I have to give grace. I need to understand it is not what I deserve but what I have been given. This means I cannot resent God for giving grace to someone else because I have freely received it myself.

Don't close this chapter of your life. If you still have the desire to get married, work toward this goal. Don't let hurt or societal norms stop you from experiencing the blessing of marriage.

Work It

Knowing the statistics are higher for a failed second marriage, we work harder because we have more to overcome. We have attitudes to unlearn and prejudices to overcome. Preparation takes longer and does not come merely by wishing things will be better next time. Don't bury your head in the sand. Face the challenges, count the cost, and do battle with your second chance!

If you are coming out of a broken relationship or marriage:

- **Give yourself time to heal.** The question in most people's hearts is what counts as enough time. Is it three months, one year, five years? I believe the answer varies for each person, but a general rule of thumb is between six months to a year. The time of healing will depend on various factors— the depth of hurt, the length of time invested in the relationship, emotional health, and even the spiritual state of the persons involved.

- **If you are coming out of an abusive relationship, seek counseling.** No person created by God deserves to suffer abuse, especially from the hands of someone who supposedly promised to love you above all else. If you have been abused,

seek counseling to help you get over the pain
and misplaced guilt. Work through the pain, so it
doesn't taint your next relationship.

❧ **Work on learning good relationships without
pressure.** A great way to recognize bad
relationships is being in good ones. As you meet
new people and make new friends without the
pressure of being in a relationship, you develop
your emotional IQ and improve your chances of
identifying a good man.

❧ **Own your part in the divorce.** The worst thing
that could happen is not to learn anything from
the failed relationship. Search your heart and
understand what you would have done differently
if you had a chance for a do-over. Your goal is
to do things right the next time around, not to
condemn yourself for past mistakes you cannot
change.

❧ **Forgive the other party.** Bitterness will only ruin
you. You cannot afford to give a past relationship
prominence in your future. An inability to forgive
is a sure indicator you are not ready for another
relationship. Bishop TD Jakes puts it this way,
"Forgiveness is a gift you give yourself." It doesn't
exonerate the other person or nullify the offense; it
is something you do because you need to let go of
your past to be able to reach toward your future!

❧ **Wait for God's best for you.** Don't run ahead
of God's plan by rushing into any and every

relationship. Leah was the older sister of Rachel, and she literally stole her younger sister's husband. I empathize with Leah and the pain she went through, waiting year after year for someone to come to claim her hand in marriage. Seven years after Jacob committed to working for the hand of Rachel, she was still alone and unloved. She went along with her father's plan to deceive Jacob by taking her sister's place in Jacob's tent. While she achieved her goal of being married and having many children, she suffered a lifetime of emotional pain in this marriage. She was married but still alone and unloved. Don't act on the human tendency to help God along. This rarely ends well, and we often find that our true happiness lies not in what we have been striving for but in the things God gives to us!

> *Our true happiness lies not in what we have been striving for but in the things God gives to us!*

You may be wondering why I have taken the time to address divorce and remarriage at this level of detail. This is not intended to encourage anyone to go ahead and file for divorce for "irreconcilable" differences. I firmly believe every marriage has a 100 percent chance of success and God can repair any brokenness if both parties are willing. After all, God promised to make even your enemies be at peace with you.

"When the Lord takes pleasure in anyone's way, he causes their enemies to make peace with them" (Proverbs 16:7).

If you are embracing the single life because you have a load of guilt from a divorce and think there is no other way out, I want to encourage you to seek counseling from mature and balanced Christians. Remaining unmarried should be a choice you take to please God, not something forced on you by societal opinion. In the same vein, if you are separated from your husband and holding on to the prestige of being married without the work involved, make a decision today. That decision may be to work on reconciliation, and where this proves impossible, let the man go. Staying in limbo is not fair to you or your husband in this case. As always, there is a myriad of issues and reasons that cannot be handled by a few lines in a book. You will need to study what God says about divorce and remarriage yourself,[9] so that you can make an informed decision. God did not create you to carry guilt over a divorce forever. He is the God of second chances.

---

9 See below for some books that deal with the subject in additional detail *Divorce and Remarriage, (3rd Ed.): Recovering the Biblical View* – William F Luck
Marriage, Divorce and Remarriage – Kenneth E Hagin
Divorce and Remarriage in the Church – David Instone-Brewer
Divorce and Remarriage in the Bible – David Instone-Brewer

FOR THE WIDOW

If you have been widowed and would like to get married again, do not let other people's opinions or your personal fears stop you from taking that step. Most people seem to have an opinion on how a widow should live her life after a loss, but few do this from a position of experience.

I lost my dad when I was nine, and in the first weeks after his death, our home was filled with friends and family who came to commiserate with us. My mother had a lot of things she was expected to do, and my grandmother was there to help make sure she met the expectations of all the people around us.

At some point before the funeral, my grandmother mentioned something that my mom needed to do, to which she responded, "Is that what you did when your husband died?" My grandmother responded. "My husband is not dead."

My mom retorted, "Since it's my husband who died, would you let me do things my own way?" I share this story because all the expectations well-meaning friends and family will place on you may not be fair or reasonable. You need to be able to stand up for what is best for you and your family. Over the course of time, you may begin to crave love and companionship. You may want to be able to have sex again or try to have children. Your body did not die with your husband, and you have the same physical needs you had when he was alive. Give yourself permission to love again and remarry. Do what is best for you! God has promised beauty for ashes and the oil of joy for mourning[10]—take Him up on His offer!

---

10 Isaiah 61:3

*The younger widows should not be on the list, because
their physical desires will overpower their devotion
to Christ and they will want to remarry. Then they
would be guilty of breaking their previous pledge. And
if they are on the list, they will learn to be lazy and
will spend their time gossiping from house to house,
meddling in other people's business and talking about
things they shouldn't. So I advise these younger widows
to marry again, have children, and take care of their
own homes. Then the enemy will not be able to say
anything against them.* (1 Timothy 5:11–14 NLT)

WHAT ABOUT THE CHILDREN?

What happens if there are children in the mix? We would
be remiss if we didn't talk about the role of children in a
single woman's life, whether from a previous marriage or in
the new person you are dating.

After I lost my dad, I watched my mom raise four kids
on her own. I asked her once if she would consider remarrying and her response was reflective of the conventional
wisdom of that time, "How do I know he will not mistreat
my children?"

While a lot of women decide to go it alone after a
divorce or widowhood, it's important to make sure you are
not using your children to replace the affection of a husband. Children should not be cast in this role as they will
eventually grow up and leave home when they come of age.
If you are willing to take a calculated risk to search for a
good man who meets that criteria, dating is more difficult

as you have the children to consider. This man needs to gel, not just with you but with your children, alongside dealing with ex's, prior in-laws, and family members.

On the flip side, you may not have any children and be considering dating a man who already has children. As beautiful as Hollywood makes blended families seem, a lot of work and prayer goes into getting two preexisting families to come together as a single cohesive unit. There are various resources to help coach you through the process of building this new family unit, so do not feel you have to do this on your own when the time comes.

If you know you are unable to welcome someone else's children into your heart and home to love them as if you birthed them yourself, do not get into that kind of relationship.

A shout out to the single, never-married mothers out there. You are in an oft-forgotten group that tends to be glossed over because we don't want to talk about how you came to have children in the first place.

The most frequent assumption is a never-married mother must have been promiscuous. In my opinion, the truly promiscuous woman would know her way around to prevent a pregnancy or would abort the child if she got pregnant. We don't think about the fact it could be rape or one wrong choice that resulted in getting pregnant. But it really doesn't matter how it happened. I do not believe in closing the barn door after the horse has escaped. You do not owe me or any other nosy person an explanation.

You made the right choice to preserve a life in spite of the stigma, and for that, I salute you. Have you asked God for forgiveness if you disobeyed His Word? Once you have done that, believe He has forgiven you and move on, leaving your self-condemnation at the foot of the cross. There will always be people who will look down on you, but rest assured, this is not representative of the loving and forgiving God we serve.

> *"Therefore, there is now no condemnation for those who are in Christ Jesus"* (Romans 8:1).

IN CONCLUSION

A lot of churches have struggled with presenting a cohesive stance on divorce and remarriage over the years; which has failed people trapped in abusive and toxic marriages in favor of promoting legalism. Many women have been sentenced to a life of solitude and loneliness due to narrow interpretations of the law, resulting in many more women shunning advances by divorced men to avoid the "sin of adultery."

Grace says there is no guilt, no shame, and no pain He cannot take away

I have personally struggled with prevailing opinions on divorce and remarriage for many years. This resulted in my spending a reasonable amount of time studying the subject. Even while writing this book, I have debated within myself on whether to speak my heart or keep this under wraps, as I do not want to lead anyone into sin. I have decided to be bold and speak what I believe God has been saying all along; remarriage after divorce is possible without committing the sin of adultery.

So to all my sisters who have gone through a divorce, been widowed, or have a child born out of wedlock, I want to remind you of the miracle of grace. Grace says you can be a wife if you so desire. Grace says God is able to give you double for your trouble. Grace says God can help you excel as a single woman. Grace says there is no guilt, no shame, and no pain He cannot take away. Grace says you have not already had your only chance because I am the God of the second chance!

LIFE APPLICATION

1. What viewpoint on divorce resonates most with you? Why?

   - Viewpoint 1: Divorce and remarriage are always sinful.

   - Viewpoint 2: Divorce is allowed under two exceptions, but remarriage is always sinful.

   - Viewpoint 3: Divorce is allowed under some exceptions and remarriage allowed under those circumstances.

2. If divorced—are you emotionally ready for another relationship?

   - Have you forgiven your ex-husband?

   - Are you and your ex-husband on speaking terms?

- What do you think you might have done to prevent the divorce?

- Have you had any counseling after the divorce?

3. If widowed—are you emotionally ready for another relationship?

   - Were you happily married to your husband?

   - Have you healed from the loss of your husband sufficiently to go into a new relationship?

   - Do you still wear your wedding ring as a signal you are not interested in a new relationship?

4. Do you have any children from prior relationships?

   - What is the relationship between your children and their other parent, if living?

   - How do you speak about your children's dad when talking to them?

   - How do your children feel about your going into a new relationship?

CHAPTER

Wait—You Mean Forever?

I wish I had a crystal ball to scratch, so I could see to the end of my life and find out how certain situations would end. Sometimes I wish God would just let me know what is going to happen, so I can adjust my life. But alas, God doesn't operate that way. Instead, He calls us to walk by faith! Faith is not a magic potion that says everything we ask for will automatically be ours—faith understands the sovereignty of God, as well as the love He has for His children. I am always awed by the story of Shadrach, Meshach, and Abednego, who told Nebuchadnezzar their service to God was not dependent on things going the way they wanted it to.

> *If you throw us in the fire, the God we serve can rescue us from your roaring furnace and anything else you might cook up, O king. **But even if he doesn't**, it wouldn't make a bit of difference, O king. We still wouldn't serve* your gods or worship the gold statue you set up." (Daniel 3:17–18 MSG)

WHAT IF IT DOESN'T HAPPEN FOR ME?

Let me ask you a question I have asked myself multiple times. What happens if you never get married? The first time I asked myself this question, I had so much fear and panic at entertaining such a reality. As time went on, I realized my response was out of fear and not faith. If I am never going to get married, wouldn't I want to know that now? Would refusing to entertain the thought change this outcome? I found that facing the thought of remaining single all my life actually did the reverse. I considered what life would look like if I never married, and this helped me to overcome the fear and built up my faith.

> *Faith says, even if I do not receive the answer I want, I will continue to believe in the God who is able to answer this.*

I know you have been praying, fasting, and trusting God that marriage will happen any day now. As much as I would like to assure you that you will get married, I cannot, in all honesty, do so. Instead, it is important to know that part of waiting correctly is facing the reality that singleness may be your calling and evaluating the worst that can happen. Faith does not mean burying your head in the sand and refusing to consider other alternatives. Faith is looking at the problem and saying, even if I do not receive the answer I want, I will continue to believe in the God who is able to answer this.

Each one of these people of faith died not yet having in hand what was promised, but still believing. How did they do it? They saw it way off in the distance, waved their greeting, and accepted the fact that they were transients in this world. People who live this way make it plain that they are looking for their true home. If they were homesick for the old country, they could have gone back any time they wanted. But they were after a far better country than that—heaven country. You can see why God is so proud of them, and has a City waiting for them. (Hebrews 11 MSG)

I heard a man of God, Bishop Julius Abiola[1], teach about this in six simple points on faith, which I believe drives this home perfectly.

Walking by faith is:

1. Believing even when I don't see it.

2. Obeying even when I don't understand it.

3. Giving when I don't have it.

4. Persisting when I don't feel like it.

5. Thanking Him before I receive it.

6. Still trusting even if I don't get it.

Will you still love God if you never get married? Would you trust that He still has your best interests at heart?

---

1   Presiding Bishop, Christ Life Ministries, Brooklyn, New York

EXTREME MAKEOVER—GIRL'S EDITION

Imagine you are on the set of the popular show *Extreme Makeover*, and the host brings you up on the set and says: *"I have some news for you. I have gone into the future and seen that you will not get married for the next twenty years. My job is to find out what you would do differently and help you make plans to ensure you are able to enjoy your life without a partner. I am going to give you a tablet, and I want you to write out what you would change in your life to make you comfortable with this new reality."*

Would you do this exercise with me? Would you take a piece of paper and write down what you would change in your life if you were to remain single? I can start you off with some questions I considered for myself.

- Would you be doing the same job?

- Would you get more education?

- How will this affect where you would choose to live?

- Does this impact how you plan your vacations?

- Would you buy a new house?

- How much travel would you incorporate into your life?

- Would you go on an extended mission trip?

What would you change in your life right now? What dreams and aspirations are currently being sacrificed on the altar of marriage? I believe with all my heart that God has placed me on earth for a specific purpose, and when He calls—He equips. The fact I am not married now means I can fulfill God's purpose for my life while single. When the time comes that the lack of a partner would hinder the work He has placed in my hands; God will provide the said partner to help me fulfill my destiny. I want to encourage you to lift up those dreams and aspirations, the life changes you require, and prayerfully implement them. Don't wait for life to happen, live now and watch God make everything beautiful in its time. Living your dreams will not preclude your husband from coming, it will quickly showcase the ones who are not going in the direction God is leading you. God, not your marital status, defines your life!

> *The fact I am not married now means I can fulfill God's purpose for my life while single.*

> *And don't be wishing you were someplace else or with someone else. Where you are right now is God's place for you. Live and obey and love and believe right there. God, not your marital status, defines your life. Don't think I'm being harder on you than on the others. I give this same counsel in all the churches.* (1 Corinthians 7:17 MSG)

THREE SIDES OF THE COIN

As a young girl, I read a book about a lady missionary who I believe went to China to help spread the gospel. I remember this story because she promised God she would serve Him as a single missionary in Asia, but in the process of time, she fell in love with a good man who wanted to marry her. She wrote about how God reminded her of her promise and the pain with which she gave up this relationship to serve God. She went on to the mission field, and at the end of her life, she was perfectly content with the choice she made to remain single. My reaction to this book was probably the opposite of what she intended. For many years, I lived in fear that God would ask me to serve Him as a single woman in China. Now, many years later, I am a lot more secure that God will never ask me to do what He knows I am unable to do.

I have always found the statement Jesus made to His disciples about eunuchs in Matthew 19 to be interesting.

> *The disciples said to him, "If this is the situation between a husband and wife, it is better not to marry."*
>
> *Jesus replied, "Not everyone can accept this word, but only those to whom it has been given. For some are eunuchs because they were born that way; others were made that way by men; and others have renounced marriage because of the kingdom of heaven. The one who can accept this should accept it."* (Matthew 19:10–12)

Jesus lists three reasons why there were eunuchs in their day—these were men who had been castrated so they would remain unmarried.

1. **Nature**—They were born that way

2. **Circumstances**—They were made that way by men

3. **Choices**—They chose that way for God

Applying this logic to us women, we can identify a few reasons some of us decide not to get married. I would encourage you to evaluate your decision to stay single against these three categories—are you naturally not interested in marriage or sex as it mostly boils down to? I call this the gift of singleness.

Have you sworn off marriage based on things that have happened in your past—hurts, abuse, sickness, loss, unforgiveness, death, divorce, etc.? This is the price of singleness. Are you choosing to stay single so you can dedicate your life to God, perhaps by becoming a missionary? Let's call this the choice of singleness.

Whatever your reasons, I would encourage you to discuss your decision with trusted counselors who can help ensure you are making a well-informed decision. I recall a dear friend who insisted for years that she would not get married, but instead was going to be a missionary. A trusted friend asked why getting married would prevent her from being a missionary and challenged her to be certain this was from God and not a cop-out on her part. She realized her decision was made out of fear and was able to work through that fear until she could admit she wanted to get married. I find one red flag identifying decisions made in fear is a refusal to discuss or inability to defend the decision. You need to be secure in a decision not to get married, as it will be challenged multiple times and ways.

THE GIFT OF SINGLENESS

I wish that all of you were as I am. But each of you has your own gift from God; one has this gift, another has that. Now to the unmarried and the widows I say: It is good for them to stay unmarried, as I do. But if they cannot control themselves, they should marry, for it is better to marry than to burn with passion. (1 Corinthians 7:7)

I was talking to a friend who had gotten married, and I was trying to make arrangements to meet his wife for the first time. To my utter shock, he informed me they were already divorced. To hear him tell it, she had told multiple people that she never wanted to get married, but she was pressured into the relationship by her parents.

The challenges of a young marriage proved too much for someone who was never invested in the marriage institution. Coming from a culture like mine, it seemed incomprehensible that anyone would decide not to get married simply because they didn't want to. Where I come from, marriage is the ultimate goal for every woman, not education, wealth, or position.

As I have traveled the world and mingled with other cultures, I have seen that women who want to remain single outside the convent really do exist. I cringe at some insensitive and derogatory comments we make about women who have this gift. We call them "frigid," and refer to ourselves as "warm-blooded women," in essence stereotyping anyone who is not interested in marriage or sex as cold-blooded. Yet Paul calls it a gift—a natural ability or talent.

We do not ridicule people who have the gift of music or making money, so why is it okay to ridicule women who have a gift of singleness? On behalf of women and men everywhere who have made you feel your gift of singleness is a curse, I apologize and applaud your gift. God has specially equipped you to live the single life without some of the struggles others face, and for this, you are truly blessed.

At this point, you are probably wondering if you have the gift of singleness. This is something you will have to work out with God, but I can give a few pointers to help you narrow this down.

- Do you want to get married?
- Do you struggle with sexual desires?
- Are you uncomfortable with the prospect of a future without marriage, children or sex?
- Is your decision not to marry a result of pain or past circumstances?

If your response was no to all the questions above, you probably have the gift of singleness! As all gifts from God go, this too should be used for God's glory and the advancement of His kingdom here on earth. If your decision not to marry is the result of pain or circumstances in your past, you may be paying the price of singleness.

THE PRICE OF SINGLENESS

My mother paid the price of singleness after my father's death in their 40s. She decided to pour her life into her four children rather than risk remarrying a man who might mistreat them. Is it possible she could have met someone who would have loved us like his own? We will never know. This was a sacrifice she made to protect her children in the best way that she could.

Countless women remain single for a myriad of reasons, ranging from prior emotional or physical abuse, rape, emotional baggage from prior relationships, children, or fear. Mental illnesses, physical handicaps, developmental diseases, and other medical conditions may play into the decision to remain single. The peculiarity of being single because of other people's actions or extenuating circumstances is that this decision may change in the future. If someone told you that nobody would want to marry you or hurt you so badly you could not comprehend trusting another person in a close situation like marriage; I would recommend seeking help to overcome these scars. However, if you have made this decision and are content in your singleness, and able to face the future without fear of falling into sexual sin, live your life to the full!

THE CHOICE OF SINGLENESS

I would like you to be free from concern. An unmarried man is concerned about the Lord's affairs—how he can please the Lord. But a married man is concerned about the affairs of this world—how he can please his wife— and his interests are divided. An unmarried woman or virgin is concerned about the Lord's affairs: Her aim is to be devoted to the Lord in both body and spirit. But

*a married woman is concerned about the affairs of this
world—how she can please her husband. I am saying
this for your own good, not to restrict you, but that you
may live in a right way in undivided devotion to the
Lord.* (1 Corinthians 7:32–35)

*There was also a prophet, Anna, the daughter of
Penuel, of the tribe of Asher. She was very old; she
had lived with her husband seven years after her marriage, and then was a widow until she was eighty-four.
She never left the temple but worshiped night and day,
fasting and praying.* (Luke 2:36–37)

Maybe it's just me, but I have not met many "never
married" women close to my age, give or take a decade or
less, who decided not to get married because they wanted
to serve God. However, I have met some widows and divorcees who, like Anna, have thrown themselves into the work
of the ministry and tirelessly strive to advance the kingdom of God. The fact that I haven't met these women personally does not mean they do not exist. I daresay society
is responsible for promoting marriage over singleness for
purely practical purposes. One key takeaway from Paul's
discourse is that neither singleness nor marriage is superior
to the other. What is different perhaps is the preoccupation of singleness. Being consumed with the Lord's affairs
should be the pursuit of every woman who is currently
unmarried, be it for a season or for life.

NOT MY WILL

You are probably thinking to yourself, I don't have the gift of singleness, I am not willing to pay the price of singleness, and I certainly did not choose to be single. I am eagerly looking forward to having a home with a white picket fence and have no aversion to becoming a soccer mom. I have every desire to get married, and to further that end, I have prayed, dated, and done everything in my power to obtain my elusive MRS. degree. I have reminded God many times that He wrote, "Hope deferred is making my heart sick."[2]

I face the very real dilemma of being single "against my will." I am not going to be like the child who pretends not to want something to get it. I have plumbed the depths of my heart and identified things I am holding back from starting until I have a ring on my finger. This does not resolve the fact that, while I set out to live life to its fullest, I intend to get married sometime in the future. I think the key here is preparation, doing all I am called to do now while keeping my hope alive that my desire to be married will be fulfilled one day.

WISE VIRGIN, FOOLISH VIRGIN

Wisdom is preparing during the wait as you work toward the goal. The goal is not just marriage; it's a good marriage. It's not just a good marriage but a God marriage. A God marriage is achieved by not just marrying someone who

---

2 Proverbs 13:12

ticks "yes" in the Christian box but fulfilling God's purpose in bringing the two of you together.

One of my favorite parables in the Bible is about the wise and foolish virgins in Matthew 25:1–13.

> *At that time the kingdom of heaven will be like ten virgins who took their lamps and went out to meet the bridegroom. Five of them were foolish and five were wise. The foolish ones took their lamps but did not take any oil with them. The wise ones, however, took oil in jars along with their lamps. The bridegroom was a long time in coming, and they all became drowsy and fell asleep. "At midnight the cry rang out: 'Here's the bridegroom! Come out to meet him!' "Then all the virgins woke up and trimmed their lamps. The foolish ones said to the wise, 'Give us some of your oil; our lamps are going out.' "'No,' they replied, 'there may not be enough for both us and you. Instead, go to those who sell oil and buy some for yourselves.' "But while they were on their way to buy the oil, the bridegroom arrived. The virgins who were ready went in with him to the wedding banquet. And the door was shut. "Later the others also came. 'Lord, Lord,' they said, 'open the door for us!' "But he replied, 'Truly I tell you, I don't know you.' "Therefore keep watch, because you do not know the day or the hour."*

Wisdom is preparing during the wait as you work toward the goal.

The story fascinates me for several reasons:

- All the virgins went to meet their bridegrooms.

- All the virgins had to wait for the bridegroom.

- All the virgins fell asleep.

- The delay was not the virgins' fault—the bridegroom was late.

- What made each of them wise or foolish was the difference in their preparedness.

- The foolish virgins were still able to get oil, i.e., oil was available all along, but they missed a window of opportunity because they did not anticipate a delay.

- The oil could not be shared. The wise virgins could not rescue the foolish virgins without counting themselves out of the feast.

I don't know about you, but I want to be a wise woman while I wait for the man God has for me. I do not want to have held on for this long, only to fail just as my dream is about to be fulfilled. I know I cannot control when I will meet this husband, but I want to be certain that even if I fall asleep from the long wait, I will be ready to seize the opportunity when it finally presents itself. Wisdom is preparing for the wait! As metaphors go, I do not know what oil represents for you as a person. All I know is, you need to figure out what will keep you going if Mr. Right doesn't turn up on your schedule.

IN CONCLUSION

As we have worked through the very real possibility that
marriage may not happen for all of us, it is my hope that
you are now able to address any crippling fears and identified actions you may need to take to deal with this even-
tuality. If you are convinced that singleness is the choice
God has ahead of you, embrace your future with joy; being
convinced you are not missing out on life or settling for
less than God's best. If you are like me and still actively
interested in getting married, live in hope and prepare for
that future you dream of. The main thing is to live while
you wait, so you do not look back at life and regret all you
could have accomplished. I pray with all my heart that you
will overcome the fear of being single, as fear will drive you
to make wrong decisions. I pray that in the process of time,
you will be counted among the wise women because you
prepared while you were waiting.

> *"It's best to stay in touch with both sides of an issue.
> A person who fears God deals responsibly with all
> of reality, not just a piece of it"* (Ecclesiastes 7:18
> MSG).

LIFE APPLICATION

1. What was your reaction to the question—What if I don't get married?

2. Did you identify any changes you would make in your life right now?

3. What is holding you back from pursuing those changes?

4. In what ways have you let your marital status define your life?

5. What changes are you going to make in your life going forward?

6. Do you have the gift of singleness?

7. Do you think you are sufficiently prepared for the wait? What are you doing specifically to stay strong and focused during your period of singleness?

Wait—I'm Burning Here

So it's that time of the month, and your body is telling you it's the best time to get pregnant. Or you woke up from sleep to discover you have just had what can only be called a wet dream. You went to a romantic movie with your friends, and afterward, they went home with their spouses, leaving you all alone to wonder what to do with all that built-up sexual tension from watching the movie.

What makes this even more of an issue is that, unlike the world with their beliefs about "free love," you are striving to live for God and be pure, either to stay a virgin or to maintain your newfound commitment to keep sex within the context of marriage. The frustration comes because while your mind wants to do what is right, your body is screaming to be touched, and there are not many avenues to discuss your struggles without being labeled wanton.

Dealing with sexual frustration can become a real burden while waiting for marriage, to the point of driving women to marry just so they can participate in sex without the burden of sin.

Sex is the one thing a single woman should not be involved in. It's the dividing line between the married and unmarried. God designed sex to only be participated in within the confines of a marriage and not simply for recreational pleasure.

I often wonder why God put the Tree of the Knowledge of Good and Evil in the Garden of Eden and then told Adam and Eve not to eat of it. It seems to be God's style to give you a choice and allow you free will to choose how you will proceed. That's why God did not make sex something you are suddenly able to do once you get married. He gives us the ability to have sex and then says—wait! I created this for the confines of marriage. It doesn't matter how much you try to spin the Bible; the instruction remains clear: marriage is the only place where God sanctions sexual intimacy.

After decades of discussions on sex being taboo in the church, we are just now getting to where married women can discuss some of these issues in a safe environment. The other end of the spectrum involves discussions with young people so they can get their raging hormones under control. An oft-neglected category is the mature single woman who everyone assumes should have her act together.

While that may be true for many women, we cannot assume every woman can hold her own in this area. In my experience, I have found that many women have let down their guard in a moment of weakness, or been no match for some wolves in sheep's clothing who turned on the charm to get them into bed. Even beyond that are the women who assume it is impossible to stay pure in this day and age with the prevalence of sexually suggestive images all around us, so they go ahead and engage in sexual intercourse outside the confines of marriage.

TAKE A STAND

Settle it in your mind and heart that you want to stay free from fornication and sexual sin. As basic as that may seem, I have found in the course of talking with so many single women that it has now become "acceptable" to sleep with a guy to hold his interest in a relationship. I have even heard of supposed men of God who affirm that this is fine so long as you both are committed to marrying each other. However, this is not the standard God has called us to, for we are first believers and will answer to God for our actions. The Bible is clear that sex outside of marriage is a sin, and this must be the conviction that you and I decide to live by.

Someone once told me that the proof of self-control is not preventing yourself from taking the first cookie but preventing yourself from taking a second cookie after tasting the first one. If you have already had sex before, it's a lot harder to avoid doing it again. The fact that God forgives you, that you are able to seemingly come back from this hidden sin with few people the wiser, can lure you into believing God will turn a blind eye to sin. However, one thing is sure, the wages of sin is death (Romans 6:23); just like the death God warned Adam and Eve about. It did not all come about the moment they sinned, but unconfessed sin will kill you in a manner that might not be immediately obvious. A broken relationship with God is the worst kind of death.

> *A broken relationship with God is the worst kind of death.*

If you are currently in a relationship, demand sexual purity from whomever you are dating. Men are not animals;

they can control their sexual urges. The burden to stay pure should not rely solely on you, the man must also be invested in pleasing God. If he does not fear God enough to stay pure, there is no guarantee he will be faithful to you once you get married. Respect yourself enough to place the same value on you that God does. If Jesus willingly died for you when you wouldn't even give Him the time of day, that guy can put a ring on your finger before he sleeps with you.

Maybe your situation is not that you are blatantly trying to disobey the command to be pure. Just know that if you are emotionally involved in a relationship, sexual feelings will naturally arise. You need to put checks in place to help you stay pure because your will cannot always be relied upon to keep you out of trouble.

"Promise me, O women of Jerusalem, not to awaken love until the time is right" (Song of Solomon 8:4 NLT).

OWN YOUR SEXUALITY

I think one of the greatest challenges for unmarried women is accepting it is not a sin to have sexual feelings. I was browsing through a book recently and came across a chapter containing signs that a person is oppressed by the devil and requires deliverance. One thing listed was when a woman has a dream about sex or wakes up sexually aroused. I got to thinking about this and wondered why this was accepted as natural for men, i.e., wet dreams, but is a sign of demonic activity in women. What type of demon

only attacks women? Is it possible that some women have been tormented for years because they have the same natural urges as their male counterparts and think it is sinful? I refuse to be shamed or made to feel guilty for something I do not have any conscious awareness of because I am asleep. I do not discount the fact there are demonic influences in the world, but I daresay this is not as widespread as some cultures make it out to be.

We all fall into various categories regarding sexual activities. Some of us are virgins who long to experience what seems like a phenomenal experience, others have been and may even still be sexually active even though single. A woman's interest in sex will vary from the sexually curious to the frigid, without mentioning the mild to severe dimensions of sexual abuse that are more widespread in our society than we care to admit.

You are fearfully and wonderfully made, and acceptance of who you are is a critical part of your journey.

Given this broad spectrum of sexual interest, it's not surprising that single Christian women are reticent to share how they feel in this area for fear of being labeled loose. Whether you are highly attuned to sexual feelings, or the thought of sex never crosses your mind, know that God made each one of us different and unique. You are not a freak of nature. You are fearfully and wonderfully made, and acceptance of who you are is a critical part of your journey.

Just looking through the first chapter of the Songs of Solomon, we see multiple examples of passion expressed by the woman for her groom. I hear you when you tell me this book is an allegory of the love Christ has for the church. This doesn't detract from the more apparent meaning—this woman has a passion for her man!

> *She*
>
> *Let him kiss me with the kisses of his mouth— for your love is more delightful than wine.*
>
> *Pleasing is the fragrance of your perfumes; your name is like perfume poured out. No wonder the young women love you!*
>
> *She*
>
> *While the king was at his table, my perfume spread its fragrance.*
>
> *My beloved is to me a sachet of myrrh resting between my breasts.*
>
> *My beloved is to me a cluster of henna blossoms from the vineyards of En Gedi.*
>
> *She*
>
> *How handsome you are, my beloved! Oh, how charming! And our bed is verdant.*
>
> Songs of Songs 1:2, 3,12,13,14

The Songs of Solomon is a marvelous book that shows how God sees the union between a man and a woman as beautiful. This should be our attitude as well.

HOW FAR IS TOO FAR?

Now that we have established it's normal to have sexual feelings; we need to address what types are normal and what is a perversion. Where do we cross over into sin as opposed to normal physiological feelings? Just so there is no ambiguity, if whatever you are engaging in is a short-cut to avoid pregnancy or provide personal satisfaction of sexual needs, you have gone too far! Using these criteria, we can identify a few activities that go too far for the Christian woman who wants to stay pure.

- Oral sex is exactly what it says, i.e., sex. Even though it is not intercourse, it should be kept within the confines of marriage.

- Masturbation removes the need for a partner for sexual fulfillment, but God created sex to be between a man and his wife.

- In the same vein, heavy petting, etc. goes down the same line of trying to enjoy the thrill of sex without getting pregnant.

In summary, anything you cannot tell your future husband without shame should be avoided. Put another way, whatever you would not want your future husband to participate in with other women should be off the table for you as well.

IT'S THAT TIME OF THE MONTH

You may be wondering why the time of the month has anything to do with staying sexually pure. My intention is to
highlight situations that make us vulnerable to craving sex,
so we can keep our guard up at these times.

One of these times is when we are ovulating. Our
bodies' natural response is an increased libido, as this is
when we are most likely to get pregnant. Understanding that this is responsible for our increased sexual urges
reminds us it will soon pass. I tend to keep an eye on when
I am ovulating, so I can be extra careful to avoid sexual triggers during this vulnerable time.

Another enhancer is undoubtedly alcohol, as consum-
ing lowers your inhibitions. I do not care to argue whether
you should consume alcohol or not; you live by your con-
victions. However, you need to understand alcohol will
not help improve your decision-making skills. Multiple
instances abound in which a woman drinks a little too
much then goes ahead and sleeps with someone which she
would not have done under normal circumstances.

If you are going to spend long periods of time kiss-
ing and smooching with your boyfriend, understand you
are more likely to go too far than when you limit physical
contact.

Be careful during times you need comforting. When
you have suffered a loss or major disappointment and are
being held by your loved one, you are in a vulnerable position and more likely to accept the comfort sex may bring
in that situation.

What if you are already turned on? I have news for you. Contrary to what the media would have you believe, sex is not a physiological need required for survival. In plain terms, you will not die from unrequited sexual desires. Case in point—if you are about to sleep with someone and he says, "In the interest of full disclosure, I am HIV positive, but we can use a condom, so you are perfectly safe," I can assure you the passion you couldn't control earlier will be quickly doused.

Take a cold shower, join a gym, hold a personal prayer vigil, lock yourself in a room, sooner or later, the feelings will pass, and you will be able to face another day.

> *"For everything in the world—the lust of the flesh, the lust of the eyes, and the pride of life—comes not from the Father but from the world"* (1 John 2:16).

BUILDING CASTLES IN THE SKY

I was talking to a close friend who mentioned a disturbing conversation she had with a teenager about sex. The teenager was asking how she could make sure the guy would be good in bed without actually sleeping with him. Her fear was getting stuck for the rest of her life with a husband who would not satisfy her sexually. This test drive mentality that has permeated our society has been mostly fueled by the media, giving us a warped view of what real life is all about. Most of us are expecting to get married and spend two hours every day getting our socks knocked off by our husbands. Never mind that in the movies the girl is never menstruating when the guy wants to sleep with her, nobody has BO or a smelly mouth, never a bad day except as an early signal the marriage or relationship is heading toward trouble.

The novels are not much better. The girls first time is always with some initial pain, followed by ecstasy. There is so much passion portrayed where people willingly tear their clothes off that you as a single woman are convinced you are missing out on a crucial part of life if you are not having sex.

Having hung around married women, I have discovered sex is not as glamorous as the media portrays it. I attend all these women's meetings, and one constant topic is advising wives not to deny their husbands sex, especially after the children start coming.

On the other extreme, women who enjoy sex with their husbands do not tend to talk as much about it for modesty's sake, so maybe we are getting a skewed view. However, there is a growing trend where sex is being openly discussed in safe environments in the church. Whatever the truth may be, unrealistic expectations can drive single women to try to experience sex outside the confines of marriage. What we need to remember as singles is what happens outside the bedroom is far more important than what happens in it. No married woman will say, he threw me down the stairs the other day, but we have great sex, so we're okay. He beats the kids mercilessly, but he's great in bed. He ran through my inheritance, so we are bankrupt, but all is well in the bedroom.

On the other hand, our unrealistic expectations for the men we hope to marry also factors in. We expect the man will know exactly what to do to satisfy us, but we do not want to think about how he is expected to gain that experience. The late Pastor Bimbo Odukoya[1], a renowned relationship expert, was asked a question about the need for sexual experience before marriage. Her response was classic, "So are you going to be telling your husband during sex, no that's not how to do it? This other man I was with did it this way?" We need to hold men to the same level of accountability as God does, expecting them to live pure and, yes, sometimes come into the marriage without sexual experience or prowess. A man who cannot control his appetite before you marry him will eventually cheat on you since that is what he is trained to do.

Setting realistic expectations about men can help us navigate this single period better as we focus not on the anticipated thrill of sex, but on the whole picture.

We need to focus on what's important and understand that sex is great, but it's not larger than character, faith, and godliness in a man

Personally, I am just relieved that my husband will not need to tear off my expensive dress to prove he can't wait to get me into bed.

WHAT YOU SEE IS WHAT YOU THINK

I remember growing up as a voracious reader. I still am, and the speed at which I read still surprises people. The offside of this is that I go through books pretty quickly and am constantly looking for something else to read to

---

1   Co Pastor, The Fountain of Life Church, Ilupeju, Lagos

pass the time. I have to confess that I have made some bad decisions regarding what to read over the years. This, combined with an overactive imagination, has created images in my head that I have had to fight to erase over time. It's not enough to stay away from sex physically; you need to keep your mind pure as well. I remember reading a book by Merlin Carothers titled *What's on Your Mind*, many years ago. In it, he asks if you would be comfortable having your thoughts broadcast on a wide screen for all to see. I ask myself this question multiple times in my fight to keep my mind out of the gutter.

There is so much filth on TV, so much innuendo, that it's hard to keep the mind pure. Unfortunately, after watching some movies, you and I don't have the option of sleeping with a husband to relieve any amorous feelings raised in the movie. Music is another medium that can be so sensual it reaches into the soul and arouses emotions that should be kept dormant. Throw in some slow dancing, and you can very well find your body on fire despite your best intentions.

You need to work hard in this impure world to stay pure.

Would you take this from someone who has, and is still in the same boat with you? You need to work hard in this impure world to stay pure. Some of us are sexually curious and really want to know what's up. You need to ask yourself what you are going to do with that information. The internet has so much information that you don't really need to ask a real person anymore. Unfortunately, a lot of that information is romanticized or politicized, and there is no rating system to help you filter out what has been put there by people with an agenda. I have been in many situations where I am reading something innocent then suddenly links to pornographic sites pop up on the screen.

Don't deceive yourself into thinking that only men get hooked on porn; there are women out there who are dealing with the same issues. In fact, Pastor Jimmy Evans[2] always referred to romance novels as the female version of porn. The advent of e-readers has made it easier for us to read trash since nobody can see the cover that shows it's a trashy book.

I do not subscribe to the school of thought that only the Bible should be read, but I do believe we need more accountability on what we read. We need to ensure we are building ourselves up and not setting ourselves up for sin. Everything is lawful, but not everything is permissible. I have personally gone through times when I have turned the TV off or restricted my movies to PG-13 and below. As I have grown older, I have given a friend access to my online library to help keep me accountable for what I read. You do what works for you, but ensure you would be comfortable if what you watch, read, or listen to is broadcast to the world

> *"Finally, brothers and sisters, whatever is true, whatever is noble, whatever is right, whatever is pure, whatever is lovely, whatever is admirable—if anything is excellent or praiseworthy—think about such things"* (Philippians 4:8).

---

2   MarriageToday

HELP! ANYONE?

You might be wondering if this is just closing the barn door after the horse has escaped. The thoughts are already there, along with the struggles to keep your thoughts clean. It's important to deal with these now, as they will not automatically stop once you get married. Inappropriate thoughts will develop into fantasies and become a cancer in your marriage, requiring your husband to meet unachievable needs. Another thing about impure thoughts is they will grow in depravity, requiring more detailed erotic dreams or imaginations to satisfy your cravings. You may not be able to stop the thought from coming, but you can prevent it from taking residence in your mind. The age-old wisdom to gain control is to fight thoughts with words and words with action. You need to fight impure thoughts with God's Word. For example, I would pray using the Scripture below and personalize it to whatever I am going through at the moment.

> ~~For although they knew~~ *[Since I know] God, [I glorify]* ~~they neither glorified~~ *him as God* ~~nor gave~~ *[and give] thanks to him,* ~~but their~~ *[my] thinking [is not]* ~~became~~ *futile and [my heart is not]* ~~their foolish~~ *hearts* ~~were~~ *darkened.* ~~Although they claimed to be wise, they became fools~~ *[I am not a fool] and [have not] exchanged the glory of the immortal God for images made to look like a mortal human being and birds and animals and reptiles.*
>
> *Therefore* ~~God gave them~~ *[I cannot be given] over in the sinful desires of* ~~their hearts~~ *[my heart] to*

sexual impurity for the degrading of [my body] ~~their bodies with one another. They~~ [I have not] exchanged the truth about God for a lie, and worshiped and served created things rather than the Creator—who is forever praised. Amen.

Because of this, ~~God gave them~~ [I cannot be given] over to shameful lusts. ~~Even their women exchanged~~ [I will not exchange] natural sexual relations for unnatural ones.

* Romans 1:21–26

This is not meant to be a magic prayer you can simply deploy, and everything is suddenly ok. Staying pure requires a fight, and in many cases, you may need counseling or some other form of accountability to get things under control.

THE SECRET INGREDIENT

You did it again. Your thoughts took you to that place, and you spent time thinking about things you shouldn't have. Problems with impure thoughts and masturbation are much more widespread than most will admit, and it's important to deal with this rather than sweeping it under the rug. The allure of sexual sin makes it next to impossible to stop in your strength, but I have good news for you; God can deliver you from sin! It doesn't matter what breed of sexual fantasies you are dealing with; God is able to break their hold over you by the power of His Word. The trap of sexual sin is you have to go progressively deeper to get the same level of satisfaction you might have been enjoying previously. Sin appeals to the flesh and feels good for the moment, but the guilt and shame that follows makes us see that it brings no permanent satisfaction. Unfortunately, there is almost no safe environment for the single woman where she can be taught how to deal with sexual frustration from a body craving to be touched.

In the end, after putting in all the necessary safeguards, understand it is God who will help you stay pure—not your rules, not your wisdom, and not your determination, just your reliance on God. I remember agonizing about what I needed to do to stay pure and wondering if it would be enough. I tried to do it all on my own until I found great comfort in this Scripture.

> *This is why I suffer as I do. Still, I am not ashamed; for I know Him [and I am personally acquainted with Him] whom I have believed [with absolute trust and confidence in Him and in the truth of His deity], and I am persuaded [beyond any doubt] that He is able to guard that which I have entrusted to Him until that day [when I stand before Him].* (2 Timothy 1:12 AMP)

All of a sudden, I realized that just as I would ask God for a car or money to meet some need, I can commit my sexual purity into His hands. I know whom I have believed, and I am persuaded He is able to guard my virginity until that day when I stand before Him and commit to marrying the one He has prepared me for.

IN CONCLUSION

Sex is a topic we as Christians tend to avoid talking about in a "holy" setting. The expectation that mature, single women would suddenly be able to manage the fear that sexual frustration will be a constant companion is largely erroneous. People around us crack jokes about the need for the cranky single woman to get laid, so it improves her disposition, but we rarely acknowledge the problem in the safe environment of other Christian sisters. I encourage you today to be a listening ear to the hurting women near you, to share your stories of how you made it through those periods when you were literally in heat.

You were created as a sexual being in God's image, and your sexuality is a gift! It is a gift to be presented to the man God has prepared for you and enjoyed within the confines of marriage. This is the standard of Christ, and I say this with all the love in the world—this must be the standard for Christians. Make up your mind that you will live sexually pure before God, and don't be afraid to let other people know your struggles. God knows that in these times, we need all the help we can get to stay pure, both mentally and physically! The ultimate reason to stay pure is because of your relationship with God. Live for God as your first husband and choose to stay sexually pure for Him!

LIFE APPLICATION

1. Do you believe sex can be kept within the confines of marriage?

2. Do you believe mental virginity is as important as physical virginity?

3. What is your stand on "how far is too far" for displays of affection?

4. What tactics do you use to help deal with sexual frustration?

5. Do you need anyone to keep you accountable for your sexual purity?

6. What are your triggers (if any) for being sexually aroused?

7. What steps do you intend to take to help you stay sexually pure going forward?

Wait—About That Biological Clock?

One of my favorite movies from the 90s is the legal comedy, *My Cousin Vinny*. It was the story of a lawyer (Vinny) who, with the help of his girlfriend (Mona Lisa Vito), was trying his first case, getting his young cousin off on a murder charge. For me, one of the most memorable lines in the movie is below:

> **Mona Lisa Vito:** *Well I hate to bring it up because I know you've got enough pressure on you already. But, we agreed to get married as soon as you won your first case. Meanwhile, TEN YEARS LATER, my niece, the daughter of my sister is getting married. My biological clock is [taps her foot] TICKING LIKE THIS and the way this case is going; I ain't never getting married.*

I do believe this was the first time I heard of a biological clock, and I was tickled by the imagery of a clock counting down to an explosion, or in this case, an implosion of the reproductive system. Little did I know that in the course of time, I would need to consider the ramifications of age on my chances of having children. As Christian women, our standards are to be sexually pure while we are single. This doesn't address the very real fear that when the right man comes along, we may be at risk of decreased reproductive ability or even menopause, whether premature or expected. I would like to take some time to talk through some issues we may face and hopefully provide some guidance to help deal with the new normal ahead of us.

NOW THAT I AM OLD

I am what you may call a compulsive reader. I will even read the ingredients for toothpaste if that happens to be the only thing left to read. Combine that with an inquisitive nature, and you have someone who is constantly checking up on things to satisfy either curiosity or avoid boredom. The year I turned thirty-seven, I came across a random article that explained a woman's reproductive ability diminishes rapidly after she turns thirty-seven.

Sure enough, I noticed the length of my periods was shorter than they used to be. I was really tormented for a few months, wondering if the biological clock was dying. Finally, I took a stand and addressed the fears I had allowed to fester within me. This is not meant to be a magic formula, but I hope some aspects of my journey to peace will be helpful to you as well.

The first thing I did was confirm if my fears were real or imagined. Did I really have changes in my menstrual cycle, and if so, were these changes an indication of a bigger problem. I had been keeping a record of my menstrual cycles for years, so I would have that data available for when I was ready to have children. Browsing through the data, I saw that while the length of my periods was indeed shorter over the past few months, this was a pattern that had been repeating itself over the past years without my notice. Sure enough, a couple of months later, I was bleeding the same length of days I had been expecting. This was a wake-up call for me in some ways as I considered the ramifications of my biological clock winding down. I may not be at the stage Sarah was when she was promised Isaac, but given that I do not know when I will get married, it is not a bad idea to consider what the future may look like.

> *Abraham and Sarah were already very old, and Sarah was past the age of childbearing. So Sarah laughed to herself as she thought, "After I am worn out and my lord is old, will I now have this pleasure?" Then the LORD said to Abraham, "Why did Sarah laugh and say, 'Will I really have a child, now that I am old?' Is anything too hard for the LORD? I will return to you at the appointed time next year, and Sarah will have a son."* (Genesis 18:11–14)

As I grow older, I have considered the very real possibility I may not have biological children. Thinking logically through the issue, I have identified different options.

- I may have no issues with having children at all, some women my age are still giving birth without any intervention.

- I may be able to have children with help, such as artificial insemination or other fertility treatments.

๛ I may be able to adopt children, either from birth or older.

๛ I may marry someone who already has children

I have spent time accepting these options as my reality, and this has calmed my fears about the future. I have a responsibility to do what I can, which in this case is to pray and confess I will be able to have children when that time comes. I have learned in my walk with God that I cannot dictate how He answers my prayers. It's enough that I have told God that I want children, the rest is up to Him.

> *I have learned in my walk with God that I cannot dictate how He answers my prayers.*

FOR THIS CHILD, I PRAYED

As I mentioned earlier, I had a wake-up call about whether I was going to be able to have children, given my continued single state. My first instinct was to pray for God to regulate my menstrual cycle, so I would be more confident I was still fertile. However, I had an epiphany as I prayed about this. What I actually needed to pray for was the future children I wanted, not for a menstrual cycle. Like Hannah, I needed to ask God for my children and thank Him in advance for answered prayers.

> *"For this child I prayed; and the Lord hath given me my petition which I asked of him."* (1 Samuel 1:27).

I took this a step further. It is not enough to simply have children; it is better to have healthy children. Knowing the likelihood of developmental diseases increases with the mother's age, I included this as a prayer point and made it a habit to pray regularly for my future children. I also searched the Bible and found some Scriptures in line with the specific things I needed to pray for my children. Let me share with you an excerpt from my prayer diary that I have now begun to use regularly to secure my future:

> *"And this is what will happen: When you, on your part, will obey these directives, keeping and following them, GOD, on his part, will keep the covenant of loyal love that he made with your ancestors: He will love you, he will bless you, he will increase you. He will bless the babies from your womb and the harvest of grain, new wine, and oil from your fields; he'll bless the calves from your herds and lambs from your flocks in the country he promised your ancestors that he'd give you. You'll be blessed beyond all other peoples: no sterility or barrenness in you or your animals. GOD will get rid of all sickness. And all the evil afflictions you experienced in Egypt he'll put not on you but on those who hate you."* (Deuteronomy 7:12–15 MSG)

> *I will be a mother of children; barrenness is not my portion*
> *My reproductive organs will continue to be fruitful*
> *I trust you God for a healthy time in pregnancy*
> *Our children are free from autism, heart defects, disease, or physical handicaps*

> Our children will know and serve God for them-
> selves
> Our children are protected from childhood dis-
> eases and premature death
> Every need concerning these children is met in
> Jesus' name—financial, emotional, mental, spiritual,
> etc.
> I thank You, God, for my children

Praying for my unborn children helps me keep my eyes on God, who is the ultimate source of children. I have been a Christian long enough to know that not every Christian couple has kids without going through challenges. God is a master planner and will do what is best for us because His ways are higher than ours. We need to trust God for our future children, whether they are birthed with or without intervention, or come to us through adoption, fostering, or marriage.

God is a master planner and will do what is best for us because His ways are higher than ours.

I do not want to leave you with the impression that having regular periods is not important. You should take note of your menstrual cycles as this information is crucial to your reproductive health. If you have irregular periods, you may consider seeing a gynecologist to discuss what may be going on. This will help inform what you personally need to pray about for your future.

GIVE ME CHILDREN, OR I'LL DIE

As I prayed specifically about my reproductive health and future as a mother, I also took time out to review other options that did not involve a "miracle," but rather "process." As we discussed earlier, God cannot be put in a box! The same God who healed the woman with the issue of blood instantaneously is the same God who told the lepers to go and show themselves to the priest before they would be clean. God is Lord over both miracles and due process, and we need to trust Him through whichever He leads us through.

Medicine has advanced tremendously over the years, and there are multiple options to help an increasingly aging population of women have children later in life. With the advent of fertility treatments and artificial insemination, couples who would otherwise have been childless have been able to have children. For us as singles, these advances affect us in the following ways:

- The ability to freeze eggs and store them for future use.

- The option of using donor eggs if our eggs are no longer viable for childbearing.

- The possibility of using donor sperm to have children without getting married.

At this point, it is important to note that artificial insemination is not a guarantee of success. More than half of the procedures are unsuccessful. Age remains a crucial consideration, and costs for these procedures are relatively high. However, I would be remiss if I did not address some concerns and how these medical options can affect our outlook on life as singles.

The early purpose of freezing eggs for singles was rooted in medical issues. For example, women preparing to undergo cancer treatments now had the option to freeze their eggs before these procedures made them infertile. In more recent times, women freeze their eggs to postpone childbearing and focus on career or other personal goals.

Freezing eggs is a relatively costly procedure, with continuing costs to store the eggs until they are required for fertilization. Financial considerations aside, the dilemma before us as Christians is whether this is an act of faith or an act of the flesh. Will a child produced in this manner be an Ishmael or an Isaac? I am not a Bible scholar, but this appears to be one of those issues that call for personal discernment.

In cases like this, you need to settle within yourself what your choices in this matter are. On the one hand, it could be an expression of doubt that God would not bring a husband your way in time. You could be trying to freeze your eggs to provide a safety net, so you can still have children even if you marry later in life. On the other hand, it could be seen as an expression of faith that God will still bring a husband for you in the future.

The very fact you are freezing your eggs may be based on the certainty that you will get married at some point. Jesus never healed anyone the same way twice, so you need to ask Him what the right answer is for you! Whatever decision you take, make sure you are doing this in faith and are not substituting your trust in God for trust in frozen eggs.

> But the man who has doubts (misgivings, an uneasy conscience) about eating, and then eats [perhaps because of you], stands condemned [before God], because he is not true to his convictions and he does not act from faith. For whatever does not originate and proceed from faith is sin [whatever is done without a conviction of its approval by God is sinful].
> (Romans 14:23 AMP)

Medical advancement has also brought us the ability to use donor eggs in situations where one's eggs are no longer viable. This provides a ray of hope for older single women as it opens up a door for conception that would ordinarily be closed. In some Christian circles, the use of donor eggs is kept under wraps for many reasons. Some of these may be sensitivity to the mother's feelings or protecting the child from future ridicule or bullying. There are also Christians who will share their testimony of having a child late in life while omitting that donor eggs were required to have this child. The downside of this secrecy is some women are driven to desperate measures and marry inappropriate men just so they can have children before it is too late.

For those who believe the child will not really be yours because it came from a donor egg, I expect these same reasons may lead you to conclude adoption is not an option. It is better to know what works for you now than to resent the conception and presence of that child when it comes

later. While thinking about donor eggs, I was looking for
something analogous in Scripture and came up with the
ancient practice of concubinage practiced by the Israelites.
This practice allowed a woman to give her servant to her
husband, so any children borne of this encounter would be
her "own" children.

The account of Rachel in Genesis 30 lays this out
beautifully.

> When Rachel saw that she was not bearing Jacob any
> children, she became jealous of her sister. So she said
> to Jacob, "Give me children, or I'll die!" Jacob became
> angry with her and said, "Am I in the place of God,
> who has kept you from having children?" Then she
> said, "Here is Bilhah, my servant. Sleep with her so
> that she can bear children for me and I too can build
> a family through her." (Genesis 30:1–3)

As polygamy was outlawed and monogamy became
the order of the day, this practice became extinct in Israel
and was definitely discontinued in the Christian faith.
As concepts go, the practice of using a donor egg helps
provide an avenue for women with reproductive issues
to have children with the added advantage of avoiding
adultery.

I personally believe the ability to use donor eggs is a
blessing to couples everywhere, but taking advantage of
this will require both financial and emotional commitment
by the couple involved. For us as singles, this is another
option that may help us deal with the fear of childlessness,
so we can concentrate on the best God has for us now.

Finally, we know the option exists to artificially inseminate using donor sperm. As many of us have grown older, it is not uncommon for people to advise us to have children if we cannot get married. As Christian women determined to live for God, most of us reject this advice as it would involve the sin of fornication, with the deliberate intent of getting pregnant. In countries where this is allowed for single women, the temptation is to utilize donor sperm and artificial insemination to have a child without waiting to be married.

I want to encourage you to think about the long-term effects on the children that you would bring into the world this way. I would ask you to consider the example you would set for other single women who are trying hard to stay pure outside marriage. Though you may not have sinned to conceive the baby, you will not have the opportunity to explain to all that you had this child through medical means. You may believe you should not consider the impact of your actions on other Christians, but Scripture is clear about our responsibility to lead in a manner that does not cause others to sin.

> *"Abstain from all appearance of evil"* (1 Thessalonians 5:22 KJV).

> *"So do not let what you regard as good be spoken of as evil"* (Romans 14:16 ESV).

HERE IS YOUR SON

You may be at a point in your life where you are ready to have children even though you are not married. You may decide you are done waiting to start a home and are emotionally and financially ready for this next phase of life. Realize the presence of children may further narrow the scope of prospective husbands who may come your way. Instant families are not for everyone, and it would be a wicked thing to discontinue an adoption because you want to get married to someone in the future.

For some of us, volunteering with children in church and other organizations is a good way to get our feet wet for the responsibility of taking care of children. For women who have younger siblings, you already have a good idea of what this entails and may delve right into the next level of childcare, which is fostering or full-scale adoption

Fostering is a good way for single women to take on the responsibility of having children in their home for a time. Fostering is not available in every country, but a close equivalent can be found in which children are sent to live with wealthier relatives in a quid pro quo arrangement, providing companionship and assistance with household chores in return for basic needs like clothing, food, and education.

There is a single woman in my church who believes her ministry is to children. She has fostered many children and continues to pour the love of Christ into their lives while they reside with her. Can you imagine the impact she has had on the lives of the children who have passed through her home! The greatest gift you can give a child is introducing that child to the Savior!

Fostering can be hard emotionally as a lot of these children come from abusive or neglectful homes. When done with the right intentions, it opens up an avenue to make an impact on these kids for a period of time.

A lot of single women now have taken the plunge and gone all the way to full adoptions, either as a step up from fostering or directly. In 2016, almost 30 percent of adoptions from foster care are single parents. I will not discount the notion that children traditionally do better in a two-parent home; however, there are enough examples of two-parent homes that have abused their children that we cannot blindly hold on to this belief. Considering that two-parent homes now consist of biological parents, stepparents, or even same-sex partners, whether married or cohabiting, the demographics have changed significantly over the years.

Children are no longer automatically better off in a two-parent home. As a colleague of mine mentioned: "Just because some people have the equipment does not mean they should be allowed to have children." Sometimes they are better off with good Christian single women who will love them unconditionally. As I have mentioned before, I lost my dad when I was a child and my mother never remarried. I essentially grew up in a single parent home, and even though I missed having a resident male authority growing up, I think I turned out okay. Growing up with a single parent is far from being the worst thing that can happen to a child. Adoption can be quite expensive in developed countries and not widely accepted in others. I was privileged to have been born into an extended family that embraced adoption when it was not widely accepted.

I have learned some random things along the way which I share below.

- It still takes a village to raise a child. You cannot do it on your own, so a decision to adopt will ultimately affect your nuclear or extended family.

- A child will not replace a husband. Expecting the child to meet all your emotional needs puts unnecessary strain on the relationship.

- Keeping an adoption secret from a child is challenging when you are part of a large family. There will always be that onerous relative who takes it upon themselves to drop hints or outright tell the child they are adopted.

- Protect the adopted child legally. The fact that you are a single parent means there is no other parent to take custody if something happens to you.

- An adopted child is exactly that—your child! You don't get to return that child to the agency because that child has developmental or behavioral issues. You have committed to that child, and you need to see this through the same way you would for a child from your loins.

"Be careful. Don't think these little children are not important. I tell you that these children have angels in heaven. And those angels are always with my Father in heaven" (Matthew 18:10 ERV).

I like to think that Jesus supports adoption based on the scene that took place when He was on the cross and was going to be crucified. Jesus turned to His mother Mary (a widow) and speaking of John said, "Here is your son." I think Mary, the mother of Jesus is good company to be with, don't you?

> *"When Jesus saw his mother there, and the disciple whom he loved standing nearby, he said to her, 'Woman, here is your son'"* (John 19:26).

IN CONCLUSION

We have talked extensively about the desire to have children, but I do not want to assume this is every woman's desire. Maybe you really do not want to have kids, in which case your biological clock and its monthly alarms is more of a bother.

Some of us are ready to take the plunge now and embrace fostering or adoption. Most of us will be in the middle though, waiting to get married before starting a family. If you are fearful of being able to have kids, I hope these options have provided some clarity and reduced your fears about your biological clock.

Finally, if you find yourself pregnant out of wedlock, please do not abort that child! If you are not in a position to keep the baby, you still have the option to give the child up for adoption. I think about Mary, who must have gone through a lot of shame and ridicule when she was pregnant with Jesus. In her day, every Jewish girl prayed for the privilege of being the mother of the Messiah. I imagine some young women had used the fact that the Savior was to be born of a virgin to try to explain why they were found pregnant out of wedlock. Imagine Mary in our current day with all the options available making a decision to abort the Savior! Every child born contains a piece of eternity, a portion of the Savior, a part of the divinity. Jesus shows us that regardless of the circumstances of a child's birth, that child can grow up to be a King! Give your child a fighting chance to be everything God created her to be.

LIFE APPLICATION

1. Do you want to have children?

2. Do you keep a record of your menstrual cycle? Is this something you discuss with your doctor during your check-ups?

3. Do you pray for your unborn children?

4. What is your opinion about freezing eggs?

5. What are your biggest fears about reproduction?

6. Would you consider adoption as a single woman? What about as a viable option for starting a family after you are married?

CHAPTER

6

Wait—It's a Life Skill!

In summer 2017, my mother flew out to visit me. I arranged to meet her at the connecting airport so we could take the same flight home. As the boarding process was about to start, I realized we were probably not in the same boarding zone and decided to check her ticket. Being a frequent traveler, I have acquired a status on my preferred airline that frequently puts me in the first two zones. As suspected, Mom was in the second to the last zone. Since the rule was to board with the last zone for your traveling party, we would have to wait until nearly everyone had boarded to get on the plane.

When I informed my mom that I would wait to board with her zone, she was "offended" that she was in a much later zone. We had a good laugh about the fact that the people who boarded first were all heading to the same destination and would get there at the same time as those who boarded last. Isn't it funny how we go through life trying to be first in line, even though this has no real impact on our final destination?

I agree it's more comfortable, and I confess, gratifying, when you are honored by avoiding the wait. In the

> *We will not be able to fast-track every circumstance in life without suffering consequences.*

grand scheme of things, the final outcome hasn't changed—only the speed to get to a comfortable outcome or the length of the journey. As Christians, we have bought into the mentality that any time spent waiting is a delay to be avoided. We need to acknowledge we will not be able to fast-track every circumstance in life without suffering consequences. A suitable gestation period ensures the viability of the offspring just like learning to wait develops character.

EVERYBODY WAITS FOR SOMETHING

Following the boarding analogy further, I thought about the various reasons to get to the front of the line, or in other words, avoid waiting. I would classify these reasons under three categories—What I have, what I do, and who I am.

I might be able to avoid waiting because of what I have. This would include my ability to pay more than other passengers for a first-class ticket or recognition from the airline for the amount of money I spend over a period of time; i.e., frequency of travel. I might be able to avoid this because of what I do. I may be famous or serve in the military and, as a result, get moved to the front of the line. Finally, I could avoid waiting because of who I am, based on some characteristic that defines me such as age or a physical handicap. Everyone craves being moved to the head of the line because our basic human nature is to be preferred over others.

Pretty soon, being moved to the top of the line is no longer about privilege but entitlement. After a while, we no longer rejoice when we are fast-tracked but begin to take up arms because we believe our rights have been violated by having lost something we feel we deserve.

We forget it doesn't matter if we are first on the plane or the last one to board. The only requirement is to be in the boarding area, and the plane will not leave without you.

Society teaches that if you are wealthy enough, famous enough, or old enough, then you shouldn't have to wait.

As Christians, we are encouraged to wait for God's best for us when it comes to relationships. Growing up in church, I was taught from when I was a teenager to pray for my husband and trust God to connect us at the right time. Twenty years have passed, and I am still waiting for the right man; the bone of my bones, the husband of my heart to show up.

I have gone down the gamut in my negotiations with God. I have reminded Him of offerings I have given, of how I have put Him first with all I have. God—I am a worship leader, I teach Your Word, and I am working hard in Your house. I even remind Him of the practical by letting Him know I am a mere mortal and need to get married soon so I don't fall into sexual sin. When I sense myself getting angry and bitter, I remind myself that marriage is a privilege, not a right.

> **Waiting is a life skill that every Christian needs to embrace to make it through life successfully.**

All that I am, what I have done, even my very existence, is in God. As Paul eloquently put it: *"For in him we live and move and have our being.' As some of your own poets have said, 'We are his offspring'"* (Acts 17:28).

When I gave my life to God, I did it without conditions. It wasn't a case of, "God, I will serve You if You meet all my needs and give me a husband when I am twenty-five." It was, "God, I will even if you won't." I gave my life to God unequivocally. Everything after that is a privilege.

Waiting is a life skill[1] that every Christian needs to embrace if they are to make it through the journey of life successfully. Given the fact that we will all wait, we should have a plan we can employ for waiting. There are so many approaches to developing a strategy out there, but we will approach this by asking ourselves four basic questions—Why, What, Who, and How. For example, I ask myself variations of these questions to arrive at the heart of the matter.

Over the next few chapters, I would like to explore key elements of this strategy with you. The end goal is for you and I to develop a set of values and translatable actions that will help us weather the season of waiting ahead of us.

- Why do I want to be married?
- What am I expecting from marriage
- Who am I expecting to marry?
- How am I preparing to be married?

---

1 Life skills are abilities for adaptive and positive behavior that enable humans to deal effectively with the demands and challenges of life. https://en.wikipedia.org/wiki/Life_skills

WHY

DO I WANT TO GET MARRIED?

Why is it important for me to get married? What are the reasons behind my desire to get married? This tells me my desired purpose for marriage.

WHAT

WHAT AM I EXPECTING FROM MARRIAGE.

What are my expectations that I hope will be fulfilled when I get married? This helps solidify the vision for my marriage.

WHO

AM I EXPECTING TO MARRY?

What are the characteristics I am looking for in the man that I intend to marry?

HOW

AM I PREPARING TO BE MARRIED?

What steps am I taking to be ready for marriage? This gives me an action plan for things that are important to do while I am in my waiting season.

WHY DO I WANT TO GET MARRIED?

I had a colleague who really liked Akon's 2004 hit—*Lonely*. He would play it on repeat and even went so far as to get an album that had different styles of the same song in what I was convinced was a concerted effort to drive me up the wall. I am very quick to pick up tunes, and this song would play over and over in my head until I could hear it in my sleep. I really thought the words were depressing enough to drive someone to suicide. I learned to survive by replacing the lyrics to mean the exact opposite. *Lonely, I am not lonely. I have somebody to call my own* (complete with the ooh at the end).

Loneliness is pandemic. It strikes regardless of age, looks, height, weight, or social status. Nobody wants to spend the rest of their lives alone. Images perpetuated by the media seem to drive home the myth that the cure for loneliness is relationships. When was the last time you saw a car ad featuring a single woman? Jewelry stores rarely show a single woman buying jewelry, making you wonder if single women ever buy jewelry for themselves. The constant drive to become two has become so ingrained in us that we need to take a step back and re-examine our motives.

So why do you want to get married? On the surface, this seems like an insensitive question but stay with me as we unpack this question together. There are multiple ways to approach this, but I would like to address this in two parts namely:

- Why is marriage important? This deals with the overarching purpose of marriage.

🕊 Why is marriage important to me? This deals with
the personalized motivation for marriage.

I believe that once we start with the broader frame-
work that applies to the institution of marriage, we can
delve into how this applies to us as individuals.

WHY IS MARRIAGE IMPORTANT?

I am what you would call an incurable romantic. One telling sign is how much I love weddings! I have been a bridesmaid in about a dozen weddings, of which I have been
chief bridesmaid at least eight times. My love of weddings
is so well-known that whenever I applied for vacation, my
boss would ask, "Who is getting married this time?" Like all
true romantics, one of my favorite books of all time is Jane
Austen's *Pride and Prejudice*, a well-loved novel that tells the
story of a family with five daughters and the circumstances
surrounding three of them getting married by the end of
the book. I have read this book so many times I could recite
portions of it. I was, therefore, very happy to watch BBC's
1995 TV adaptation of *Pride and Prejudice* (featuring Colin
Firth) to see how much this matched with how I imagined
the characters to be. It brought to life various themes that
stayed with me in the book.

The father who married his wife based on her looks
and now lived in scorn of her intellect.

The indulgent mother whose sole ambition in life was
to get her five daughters—Jane, Elizabeth, Mary, Kitty, and
Lydia married.

The oldest sister Jane, who was the quintessential "girl next door" and, as expected, overcame obstacles to reach her happily ever after.

The second sister, Elizabeth, who almost missed out on a good man because of her preconceived bias.

The third sister, Mary, who eschewed company and everything feminine because she did not have beauty or talent to recommend her.

The fourth sister, Kitty, who could not stand up for what she believed in, but was influenced by whatever was the loudest voice at the time.

The fifth sister, Lydia, whose lack of discernment, combined with her desperation to marry, landed her a reprobate for a husband.

Interestingly, the scene that stuck with me the most was the double wedding scene at the end of the series; a scene not even described in the book. As the priest performs the wedding ceremony, joining the two oldest sisters (Jane and Elizabeth) with their sweethearts, he recites what I have since discovered is an excerpt from the marriage ceremony text of the Church of England's *Book of Common Prayer*.

> *DEARLY beloved, we are gathered together here in the sight of God, and in the face of this congregation, to join together this Man and this Woman in holy Matrimony; which is an honourable estate, instituted of God in the time of man's innocency, signifying unto us the mystical union that is betwixt Christ and his Church; which holy estate Christ adorned and beautified with his presence, and first miracle that he wrought, in*

Cana of Galilee; and is commended of Saint Paul to be honourable among all men: and therefore is not by any to be enterprised, nor taken in hand, unadvisedly, lightly, or wantonly, to satisfy men's carnal lusts and appetites, like brute beasts that have no understanding; but reverently, discreetly, advisedly, soberly, and in the fear of God; duly considering the causes for which Matrimony was ordained.

First, It was ordained for the procreation of children, to be brought up in the fear and nurture of the Lord, and to the praise of his holy Name.

Secondly, It was ordained for a remedy against sin, and to avoid fornication; that such persons as have not the gift of continency might marry, and keep themselves undefiled members of Christ's body.

Thirdly, It was ordained for the mutual society, help, and comfort, that the one ought to have of the other, both in prosperity and adversity. Into which holy estate these two persons present come now to be joined.

When a good marriage exists, it sets a standard of love that God can use to draw people closer to Him.

Going off the key points in the marriage ceremony, there are three primary reasons identified for getting married—children, sex, and companionship. You may argue about which is most important or if they all need to be fulfilled in each marriage. What is important is we agree each one constitutes a purpose for marriage. As society has become more and more modernized, there has

been a steady onslaught against these primary purposes
for marriage. Scientific advancements have made it possible to have sex without having children. Unfortunately,
the legality of abortions makes it possible to remove the
child if birth control fails. Society is also more accepting
of single parenting, and with artificial insemination, it is
medically possible to have children without fornicating.
In many parts of the world, more people choose to achieve
companionship by cohabiting rather than marrying. As
the traditional reasons for marriage are being eroded in
the light of modern civilization, we may be tempted to ask
if marriage is still relevant to our society today.

Marriage is still God's idea—not the bells and whis-
tles or the extravagant ceremonies, but the lifelong commitment to another person. Marriage is one of the earliest
institutions God created, showing it was and still is an
important part of His design for society. I think God loves
marriage because it is such a great picture of the love Jesus
has for the church. Sin and perversion may have distorted
the view of marriage in the world, but I sincerely believe
that when a good marriage exists, it sets a standard of love
that God can use to draw people closer to Him.

*"Let marriage be held in honor among all, and let
the bed be undefiled: but God will judge the sexually
immoral and adulterers"* (Hebrews 13:4 WEB).

WHY IS MARRIAGE IMPORTANT TO ME?

Perhaps the bigger question is, why is marriage important to me? What is my motivation for wanting to get married? Various things motivate people to get married; love, protection, social standing, financial considerations, health insurance, legal standing, immigration, and even ministry. Most of us would say that love should be the deciding factor. However, I know a lot of people who have arranged marriages. Most appear to be perfectly happy with their choice. In some cases, they show more respect and consideration for each other than those in "love" marriages.

Even in Scripture, we have all types represented. Jacob loved Rachel and worked fourteen years to marry her. Ruth needed the security of a home and asked Boaz to marry her. Joseph married Asenath, the daughter of Potiphera, to cement his political standing in Egypt. I have lived long enough to know that not all marriages motivated by love succeed and not all marriages motivated by other considerations fail. What is important is your acknowledgment of what drives you, as this will dictate your subsequent actions. So long as both parties are aware of the true motivation for marriage and are willing to go on with their eyes wide open, this is fine. Remember, it is not as important to marry who you love as it is to love who you marry. As the famous line from *Fiddler on the Roof* goes, "A bird may love a fish, but where would they live?"

Understanding the why will not only help you gain clarity on your motives, it will help you identify disparities in a potential spouse's motives. For instance, if you decide you are only marrying for love and a suitor is only

interested in companionship, you will need to evaluate if this will work for you as a couple. Another advantage of identifying your why is it helps bring to light things you may need to address. If your sole purpose for getting married is financial, you may need to ask if you are putting a man in the provider position which God should be occupying. Answering the why question naturally leads up to the next question, which is the "What."

WHAT AM I EXPECTING FROM MARRIAGE?

A friend of mine told me about an experience as she moved into a new apartment for law school. There was another lady in the room, and she asked her who she was. The lady responded, "I am Mrs."

After waiting in vain for a name to follow the title, she realized that was all the introduction she was going to get, a statement alerting her that the woman was married. I don't pretend to know why this lady responded in this fashion, but it got me thinking about how much of my identity is tied up in marriage. Am I trying to get married so I can be respected? Is marriage a badge of honor I am hoping to wear so people will treat me differently? Is my self-worth tied up in someone thinking I am valuable enough to become his wife? Do I, in the recesses of my mind, expect marriage to be a superior state to singleness? Has marriage become a goal or accomplishment, something to merely add to my list of achievements on my personal scorecard?

I find it helpful to think through all the things marriage would not do for me, so I can keep my expectations clear. Some of these are shared below.

MARRIAGE IS NOT...

1. **Marriage is not a prerequisite to heaven.** With the importance we attach to marriage, it is great to remind ourselves that Angel Gabriel will not be checking for wedding rings at the golden gate. When all is said and done, our goal is heaven, and we must remember we have access to heaven through Jesus and through Him only.

2. **Marriage is not always essential to your life ministry.** God is a God of provision, and what that means to me is He will not ask you to do something without providing what you need to do it. If I am not married right now, it means the work God has placed in my hands does not require being married now. You and I have a responsibility to fulfill our destiny, even if we don't get married. You give your all to fulfilling God's will, and if marriage is a need, He will fill it.

3. **Marriage is not a right; it's a blessing.** I get it. We all have the preconception that if we serve God faithfully, He will give us a good husband. As time goes by, that certainty becomes resentment, and it's disconcerting to see how many faith-filled women remain single or have failed marriages. One truth I keep reminding myself of when I get frustrated is Jesus died for me on the cross of Calvary. If I place that on the scale and try to match it with all the good works I can possibly think of, I could never tip the scale to where God owes me anything. If Jesus

does not do anything else for me, He has already done more than enough by dying for me. While I know God loves me and wants to continue to bless me, I ask with an attitude of thanksgiving, a humility that acknowledges marriage is a blessing I cannot demand but rather request from the giver of all good things!

4. **Marriage is not the answer to all of life's problems.** Far from solving all your problems, marriage will add its own dimension of issues that need to be addressed. I might be going through life now, thinking that marriage will solve my financial woes, remove loneliness, and help me to avoid sexual temptations! The truth is challenges may change, but they will remain. This is the essence of life; we are either coming out of a battle or going into one. There is no such thing as happily ever after if you keep the tape rolling long enough. When I attach a larger than life image to the marriage state, I remind myself TV is not real, that a novel is a figment of someone's imagination, real life is messier and stranger than fiction, and God is the answer to all my problems!

5. **Marriage is not a reward for the holier Christian women.** The women who are married now do not have a front row seat in the holiness row. Marriage is not a measure of who loves God more, prays better, or works more for God. God doesn't love married women more or think they love Him more. God gives to each one of us what we need to fulfill His plans for our lives.

Now that we have cleared up some unrealistic expectations about marriage, we need to bring this home to ourselves. Understanding what you are expecting from marriage will help determine what you need to give to get what you want!

Are you expecting love out of a marriage? Be prepared to sow love so you can reap the same.

Are you expecting respect? Start to learn respect for other people if this is a challenge for you!

Do you want children? Practice with the many children available in your area!

Is your dream a home full of laughter? How are you cultivating laughter around you now?

My mother always said she wanted her home to be a place where others would find comfort and sustenance. I knew she achieved this when her sister's ex-husband showed up late one evening with a couple of friends. They were in town for a meeting and couldn't get a place to eat. He confidently told them, "My former sister-in-law will feed us," and she did!

Identify what you want from marriage and hone the skills you need. Remember—you will reap what you sow!

IN CONCLUSION

Waiting is not the easiest thing to do, especially when it has been going on for a long time. Having a strategy to deal with waiting helps maintain clarity on why we are waiting, as well as what we are waiting for. I encourage you to take some time to plumb the depths of your heart to uncover unrealistic expectations that will only set you up for disappointment and failure. In the next chapter, we will discuss the "Who" in marriage, as we take a closer look at the mental images we have on who we would love to get married to.

LIFE APPLICATION

1. What is your attitude about waiting? Are you one to wait patiently or do you take actions to be at the top of the line?

2. How has your attitude about waiting affected your singleness?

3. Which of the four strategy questions resonates most with you and why?

   - Why do I want to get married?

   - What am I expecting to get out of marriage?

   - Who am I expecting to marry?

   - How am I preparing to be married?

4. What wrong expectations of marriage have you uncovered? How do you think you developed that expectation?

Wait—Who am I Waiting For?

I remember sitting with some people and talking about how much money doctors would earn after completing their specializations. As a natural build up to that conversation, I asked if there were any Christian doctors going through their fellowship program that they would be willing to introduce me to. As ears perked up, I added my other requirements—he should be left-handed and speak with a British accent. Needless to say, this was the beginning and end of the search committee's efforts to find me a husband!

We all have mental images of who we see ourselves getting married to. The more organized among us create a list of characteristics they would like to have in the person they want to marry. Multiple anecdotes from our married friends have convinced us their images did not always match up to who they ended up falling in love with. People will give advice from both extremes of the spectrum; make a list, don't make a list, and have solid points to back up their stance. I think the answer is somewhere in the middle and somewhat dependent on your personality. Making a list in itself should not be the issue, it should be what you do with it and blind adherence to the list.

You see, if you didn't have any basic requirements for who you want to marry, you could get married today. If you place an ad on Facebook, there is always one man out there who is able and willing to marry you at the drop of a hat. I know this is an extreme example, but I want to stress the point that over time, you have developed preferences that you admire in prospective suitors. This is your inner barometer that makes you say, "I don't think we will fit" when you meet that guy on a blind date. It's the traits an astute matchmaker sees when they try to set you up with someone else. It's the preferences you select on eHarmony or Christians Mingle.

Thinking through your mental image of who you want to marry will help in three ways:

- It will help you identify what is important to you.

- It will help you identify mindsets and biases you need to change.

- It will help you identify who you need to be to attract what is important to you.

The ultimate goal is not to come up with a list of what you want in a man; it is to come up with a picture of what you need to be to become the wife of that man.

Let's go through what I would call a requirements gathering exercise using the following five-step process. This is guaranteed to make you a great CATCH (I couldn't resist it).

C ompile a list of the traits or characteristics of
the man you want to marry.

A lign your requirements with their appropriate
categories.

T ransform your list into behaviors you will adopt
to attract your desired requirements.

C hange your behavior to become the woman you
need to be.

H ope in God as the ultimate judge of what is
best for you.

COMPILE A LIST OF THE TRAITS OR CHARACTERISTICS OF WHO YOU WANT TO MARRY

Imagine you have been given carte blanche to design the man you would like to marry. There are no restrictions, anything you describe is possible. Write down everything you can think of without trying to determine if it is silly or unimportant. This is your private list so go all out. This list will be important not just for what you write, but also for what you do not write.

Using my previous example, a sample list is below.

I want a man who is nice.

I want a man who is rich.

I want a man who is tall.

I want a man who is a doctor.

I want a man who is left-handed.

I want a man who speaks with a British accent.

ALIGN YOUR REQUIREMENTS WITH THEIR APPROPRIATE CATEGORIES

Now that you have a list, you need to sort the wheat from the chaff. I would typically think about three categories to classify the list listed below.

- **Deal Breaker Column**—Things that are absolutely crucial to see in a man I would marry.

- **Wish List Column**—Things I would love to see but are not crucial.

- **God Don't Do This To Me, Nevertheless not My Will but Yours Be Done Column**—This is for things I would rather not see in a prospective husband.

Deal Breakers

What are your deal breakers? To help determine what those really should be, let me tell you about the Serial Killer test. This is simply looking at each item on your list and asking if a serial killer can do that as well. The aim is to help you sift out what is crucial to your purpose from what you strongly desire. Continuing our example from before, my requirements were:

I want a man who is nice.

I want a man who is rich.

I want a man who is tall.

I want a man who is a doctor.

I want a man who is left-handed.

I want a man who speaks with a British accent.

Well, can a serial killer do that?

A serial killer can be nice.

A serial killer can be rich.

A serial killer can be tall.

A serial killer can be a doctor.

A serial killer can be left-handed.

A serial killer can speak with a British accent.

I acknowledge this will not be fail-safe, but it will help tease out the meatier parts of your requirements. Let me share a few of my deal breakers with you. My future husband must have a personal relationship with God. He must not be physically or emotionally abusive. He must be single (we have to add this now in the times we live in).

While it is possible to be deceived about this, it should be deceit and not turning a blind eye to these traits.

Each of us will have deal breakers, i.e., things we are not willing to accept in a spouse. This is what makes us unique as human beings and that's perfectly fine. The deal here is to ensure your deal breakers look like something God would write, rather than long-standing biases.

Wish List

Most of our requirements will fall into this list—things we would love to have or, at least, think we want to have. This list also tends to evolve and shorten over the years as we refine what is important to us. For me personally, singing is a big part of who I am and the thought of not being able to share that with my husband is scary for me. Rather than obsess about it, I simply put it on the list and ask God to do what's best for me.

Until a few years back, one trait on my list was my husband must be able to kill a chicken. This came from an experience I had when I was in college. Growing up, my mother had poultry, and I was petrified of the birds. At the end of each year, the chickens would be fully-grown, and we would need to slaughter a good number of them and store or give them away as gifts. Over the years, I would pay for anyone who was willing to help me to kill my allotted birds until my mom felt she had let it go on for long enough. On the 31st that year, she stood over me and made me kill my first and last chicken to date. I was so traumatized by the experience that I did not speak for the next six hours! To make sure I would never go through that again, I determined my husband must be able to kill a chicken because I was not going to do it. Since moving away from home, the likelihood of anyone presenting me with the gift of a live chicken is practically nil, so I have let that requirement slide.

I share that story because I have found it's important to ask myself the reason some of these choices show up on my list. As I become more and more in touch with who I am as a person, I am able to refine my list to be more concise and impactful.

God Don't Do this to Me, Nevertheless not My Will but Yours Be Done

Finally, some requirements you really do not want in your husband but cannot justifiably put them in the deal breaker column. One of these for me was not speaking English well. I am a "Silently-correcting-your-grammar" kind of person. It became silent when it affected my relationships with friends. It stayed silent because I realized my grammar wasn't perfect anyway. As much as I tell myself it shouldn't matter if I meet a good man and his command of English is poor, right now it still does. I can understand when English is a second language, but if you come from an English-speaking country, I think it's just a lack of effort. I do not want to spend the rest of my life silently correcting grammar in my home or telling the kids—"Don't say it like Dad does." However, I am willing to overlook this if all the other good far outweighs this "flaw".

Some things that fall into this category relate to the types of people we see ourselves married to, what we believe we will accept while married, or what we believe will signal the end of a relationship. This ranges from the acceptability of inter-racial marriages, or even inter-tribal marriages when you come from a culture like mine. What level of education are you willing to consider and why? The key here is not that you are wrong in wanting to marry someone who looks like you, it's identifying why it is your choice. Once you isolate your reasons for some of these choices, you can evaluate if these are preconceptions you need to remove and replace in your mind

I have heard people give testimony that a forty-year-old woman married a man who had never been married before. I always ask myself if it is a greater testimony to marry someone who has never been married before. Did Rachel or Rebekah have a better testimony than Ruth, Bathsheba, or Abigail? What underlying biases do I have to overcome?

- Would I consider a man who has prior children out of wedlock?

- Is a widower or divorcee fair game?

- What are my thoughts about someone from a different culture?

- Am I willing for my husband to be younger than I am?

I am convinced there is no right or wrong answer to most of these preconceptions. What is key is to be open to where God is leading you. Don't shut a door God is opening

just because it doesn't fit in with your preconceived notions
of what your spouse should look like.

> *About noon the following day as they were on their*
> *journey and approaching the city, Peter went up on*
> *the roof to pray. He became hungry and wanted some-*
> *thing to eat, and while the meal was being prepared,*
> *he fell into a trance. He saw heaven opened and some-*
> *thing like a large sheet being let down to earth by its*
> *four corners. It contained all kinds of four-footed ani-*
> *mals, as well as reptiles and birds. Then a voice told*
> *him, "Get up, Peter. Kill and eat." "Surely not, Lord!"*
> *Peter replied. "I have never eaten anything impure or*
> *unclean." The voice spoke to him a second time, "Do*
> *not call anything impure that God has made clean."*
> *This happened three times, and immediately the sheet*
> *was taken back to heaven.* (Acts 10:9–16)

Finally, check to make sure your list matches up with
where God is leading you personally. God is not the author
of confusion. If He is calling you to be a missionary to
India, you probably need to be trusting God for a man who
wants to or is already a missionary to India.

My brother told me many years ago as I was leaving for
the U.S., "Do not worry. God will not lead you away from
His provision. If He is leading you to settle in the U.S., your
husband is either there or on the way there."

> *"And he said, Blessed be the LORD God of my master*
> *Abraham, who hath not left destitute my master of*
> *his mercy and his truth: I being in the way, the LORD*

led me to the house of my master's brethren" (Genesis 24:27).

TRANSFORM YOUR LIST INTO BEHAVIORS YOU WILL ADOPT TO ATTRACT YOUR DESIRED REQUIREMENTS

Randy Pope's *Finding Your Million Dollar Mate*[1] has had a profound impact on my life. In this book, he contrasts the world's approach to dating with the spiritual approach to dating: one ending in a vicious cycle and the other leading to edification. For me, the focal point of this book was you don't find the right person, you become the right person. Writing the list above is not about giving you a list of criteria to judge every potential suitor. It is about giving you a list, so you may examine yourself and effect the change you desire.

If I want a deeply spiritual man, I must be deeply spiritual myself.

If I want a rich man, I must be an asset to a rich man.

Maybe it has nothing to do with your list at all. It could be something as basic as, if I want to get married and stay married, I need to deal with my temper.

It reminds me of a game show on GSN called *Baggage*. The gist of this dating show was three contestants each had three pieces of baggage, small, medium, and large. The main contestant they were trying to get on a date with would then eliminate them based on the baggage that was a deal breaker for him/her. The kicker was, at the end of the show, the last

1 Northfield Publishing, 2009

> **While you cannot control the other person, you can make a change in your life now.**

contestant standing would have to evaluate the baggage of the main contestant to see if it was something they could accept. I guess the point to this is you can stand and evaluate other people's baggage, but you should never forget they also get to evaluate yours. While you cannot control the other person, you can make a change in your life now.

I believe the question you need to ask yourself and answer as honestly as you can is this; If I find a man with these characteristics, would I make his life better or worse? Would I be a help meet for my husband!

CHANGE YOUR BEHAVIOR TO BECOME THE WOMAN YOU NEED TO BE

I tend to build up libraries pretty quickly. I wish I could tell you I always read the best books but that would be an untruth. There are two things I measure myself on and where I come short at times. One is the tendency to buy books and not read them. This rarely happens with novels, but I found a lot of the self-improvement books I bought end up on the shelf, partially read or not read at all. The other issue is reading the book but not doing anything with the advice in it. The book of James refers to this as deceiving myself. It would be a tragedy if we went through this exercise and you never made any changes in your life. Change your behavior to become the woman you need to be!

"Do not merely listen to the word, and so deceive yourselves. Do what it says" (James 1:22).

Change is hard! It involves getting rid of old habits and replacing them with new ones and frankly, this is rarely fun. I often suffer from a lack of motivation to change, and I have learned to ask God for help with this. One of my favorite all-time Scriptures is Philippians 2:13. I am constantly asking God to help me to want to do what pleases Him!

"For it is God who is producing in you both the desire and the ability to do what pleases him" (Philippians 2:13 ISV).

Over the years, I have asked God to bring people my way who have character traits similar to my future husband. My prayer was for God to refine and help me deal with potential issues early. I know this will not remove the potential for conflict, or should I say growth between us as a couple. I am simply looking for a head-start on issues I will have to deal with in any event. I want to be a Proverbs 31 woman, so my husband has full confidence in me and lacks nothing of value. I want to be a wife of noble character, and I believe that training doesn't have to start when I get married but can start now.

Issues I need to learn to deal with may not always be something that goes against God's Word; it could be something as simple as learning to do things another way. I have been single for a while, and am pretty set in my ways. It does me good to constantly grow in my capacity to accommodate other people and learn different approaches to issues. We will talk more about the mechanics of how to prepare to be a good wife in subsequent chapters. Suffice to say that the time to change is now and not later. It will save you a world of hurt down the road.

> *"He who finds a wife finds what is good and receives favor from the Lord"* (Proverbs 18:22).

> *"A wife of noble character is her husband's crown, but a disgraceful wife is like decay in his bones"* (Proverbs 12:4).

> *"A wife of noble character who can find? She is worth far more than rubies. Her husband has full confidence in her and lacks nothing of value. She brings him good, not harm, all the days of her life"* (Proverbs 31:10–12).

HOPE IN GOD AS THE ULTIMATE JUDGE OF WHAT IS BEST FOR YOU

When all is said and done, the crux of the matter is often how much you trust God to direct you to the man of your dreams. The package does not always reflect the treasure inside, and on the flip side, the package may be covering up a lot of fluff and issues. No matter how much we identify wish lists and change items, we must learn to submit them to God and be sensitive to His leading.

"Many are the plans in a person's heart, but it is the LORD's purpose that prevails" (Proverbs 19:21).

I listened to an interview with worship pastors Kari Jobe and her husband, Cody Carnes,[2] where they talked about how they had been friends for years and she never considered him for marriage. She said one thing she believed was her husband would have green eyes and Cody did not. Well, Cody moved to Arizona as worship pastor for the Gateway Church, and when he came back to visit, she realized his eyes had turned green (attributed to the extreme exposure to the Arizona sun).

This, more than anything, finally convinced her that God was not only orchestrating the union but He cares about our preferences.

No matter how much we identify wish lists and change items, we must learn to submit them to God and be sensitive to His leading.

Everything may not look the way we want it to. We may not get everything we ask God for, but when we trust God to do for us what we cannot do for ourselves, to see beyond our earthly limitations to a future that only He can see; He will surprise us with the best of what we need as only God can do!

"'For I know the plans I have for you,' declares the Lord, 'plans to prosper you and not to harm you, plans to give you hope and a future'" (Jeremiah 29:11).

2   Interview with Brian and Jenn Johnson on Worship, Their Marriage Testimony and Tragedy at the Bethel Conference Heaven Come 2016

IN CONCLUSION

All our prior strategy questions, the "Why," the "What," and the "Who" culminate in actions for the "How," which we will discuss over the next few chapters. Our overarching goal is to become more and more like Jesus as we prepare for the man He has kept us for all the while.

LIFE APPLICATION

1. Do you agree with the practice of preparing a list of characteristics you would like in your future husband? Clarify your positions.

2. If you created a list and applied the Serial Killer Test, what percentage of your list ended up in the three categories? What does this teach you?

3. What changes are you going to make in your life today to help you prepare to be the woman you are called to be?

CHAPTER

8

Wait—It's an Action Word!

Fairy tales! Those amazing stories that tell about insurmountable odds and amazing feats! You know you are about to hear one when it starts off, "Once upon a time…" The author takes you into a creative world of make-believe which always end with, "and they lived happily ever after— The End!" I personally loved Cinderella, Sleeping Beauty, Beauty and the Beast, Puss n' Boots, and Snow White. The sad thing about fairy tales though is they are not real. As we grow older, we substitute them for Hallmark movies or other chick flicks and live vicariously through them. But life is not a fairy tale. There is no fairy godmother about to wave a magic wand and turn you into a Cinderella.

I was reading through some quotes on waiting and found one by Ariana Grande that struck me. *"I like Aurora, 'Sleeping Beauty,' because she's just sleeping and looking pretty and waiting for boys to come kiss her. Sounds like a good life— lots of naps and cute boys fighting dragons to come kiss you.*[1]*"*

---

1   Read more at: https://www.brainyquote.com/quotes/ ariana_grande_571276

Doesn't this describe us sometimes as we sit and wait for that man to come, without giving any thought to what that translates into for us? We can talk about why we want to be married and what we expect to get out of marriage all day long. We can describe to the toenail the type of man we want to spend the rest of our lives with. But until we can translate these into the "How" of preparing for marriage—they will remain dreams or concepts that are mere castles in the sky.

> *Marriage involves the whole being, and it is fitting we should consider preparing our total being—spirit, soul, and body.*

Marriage involves the whole being, and it is fitting we should consider preparing our total being—spirit, soul, and body.

"May God himself, the God who makes everything holy and whole, make you holy and whole, put you together—spirit, soul, and body—and keep you fit for the coming of our Master, Jesus Christ. The One who called you is completely dependable. If he said it, he'll do it!" (1 Thessalonians 5:23 MSG)

PREPARE YOUR SPIRIT

The spirit is arguably the most important part of the Christian woman. This is the part of us that communicates with God. I will not spend time talking about spending time in the Word, maintaining a habit of fellowship with God and other believers, or other basic tenets of our faith. We should be doing these things already in our walk with God since we need to know God for ourselves.

Paul, talking to the Corinthians, was clear about the preoccupation of single women, which is to be devoted and completely sold out to God in both body and spirit. I take this to mean we should be consumed with the things of God; spending time in His presence, going out on mission trips and outreaches, working tirelessly in our local churches, and volunteering to help where needed. This is the time to lay it all on the altar because when your husband comes and children follow, life changes and your attention needs to be divided.

> But a married man is concerned about the affairs of this world—how he can please his wife and his interests are divided. An unmarried woman or virgin is concerned about the Lord's affairs: Her aim is to be devoted to the Lord in both body and spirit. But a married woman is concerned about the affairs of this world—how she can please her husband. (1 Corinthians 7:33–34)

Beyond the preoccupation of the single woman, we can also pray to prepare spiritually for marriage.

The Message translation for Romans 8:22–28 tells us how prayer helps us in the waiting. Though we cannot see the future, God can; and it is a smart move to put Him in charge of getting us to the end goal!

All around us we observe a pregnant creation. The difficult times of pain throughout the world are simply birth pangs. But it's not only around us; it's within us. The Spirit of God is arousing us within. We're also feeling the birth pangs. These sterile and barren bodies of ours are yearning for full deliverance. That is why waiting does not diminish us, any more than waiting diminishes a pregnant mother. We are enlarged in the waiting. We, of course, don't see what is enlarging us. But the longer we wait, the larger we become, and the more joyful our expectancy.

Meanwhile, the moment we get tired in the waiting, God's Spirit is right alongside helping us along. If we don't know how or what to pray, it doesn't matter. He does our praying in and for us, making prayer out of our wordless sighs, our aching groans. He knows us far better than we know ourselves, knows our pregnant condition, and keeps us present before God. That's why we can be so sure that every detail in our lives of love for God is worked into something good. (Romans 8:22–28 MSG)

PRAY FOR A SPOUSE

Perhaps the first thing to do is to pray for a spouse. Seems pretty basic, but a lot of us never take the time to do this. One of the most difficult things I had to do was to ask God if He wanted to me to get married. I took some time during one of the corporate prayer and fasting times at church to ask God the question because it would determine my approach toward the remainder of my life. I had to keep my heart open to hear the answer, knowing it could be something I did not want to hear or accept. On the last day, God gave me a word that has been my mainstay for the past few years. I pray this Bible verse frequently because it is God's promise to me. When my heart gets weary, I remind myself that God has never failed me yet—and I hold on a little longer.

It's also important to pray you will recognize your spouse when he comes. God is able to reveal the Jacobs in Esau's clothing when your eyes have grown dim. He can show a Rebekah it is time to water a stranger's camels, so she can be led to her Isaac. He can bring a Rachel to the well to meet her Jacob. God can bring a Ruth to glean in a field owned by her Boaz. God can do all this and more as we trust Him to bring His Word to pass in our lives.

PRAY FOR YOUR SPOUSE

Once you have established in your heart that God wants you to have a spouse, then pray for him. You may wonder what to pray for, but it's a great habit to get into now. After all, you will be praying for him for the rest of your lives together, so why not start now. When I pray for my husband, I typically pray something like this:

> I ask God to bring the two of us together. I pray for his walk with God—if he is listening to God that he will find me faster. I pray he keeps growing and doesn't grow content with being mundane. I bless the work of his hands—that God will surround

him with favor as with a shield. I pray he will be successful at work and rely on God for promotion. I pray God will lift up his head and move him forward. I ask God to help him stay pure in the midst of sexual temptation. I pray God will deliver him from seductresses and pornography and all sorts of sexual sin. I pray that if he has fallen, God will lift him up and deliver him from the clutches of the enemy. I lift up his nuclear family and the children God will give the two of us. I pray he will be a good father who will command his children in the way of the Lord. I pray he will not repeat the mistakes of his parents but will learn from God what it means to be a good father. I pray God prepares him to be the husband I need him to be. I ask God to bring people his way who will help him deal with things that would cause friction between us. That way, he has a head start on dealing with my quirks and vice versa.

The practice of praying for your spouse reminds you he is an actual person and that a relationship is as much spiritual as it is physical. Start to fight for your husband in prayer. I promise you no prayer goes unanswered. God is working to answer whatever prayers are lifted up to him!

PRAY AS A SPOUSE

It's not enough to pray for him; you need to pray for God to help you to become a good spouse. The same way you need him to be a good man, he needs you to be a good wife. Pray to become the woman he deserves, the gift of God to him. The Proverbs 31 woman is a paragon most of us only aspire to. She cooks, cleans, trades, and she does everything! It's easy to set her up as an unattainable standard to emulate. Two things summarizes bringing her to the level where you and I can relate. She is a woman of noble character, and she is a woman who fears the Lord! *"Who can find a virtuous and capable wife? She is more precious than rubies"* (Proverbs 31:10 NLT).

I like the way the New Living Translation puts it—"a virtuous and capable wife." We need to ask God to help us live righteous, for this is our mandate as Christians. We need to ask God to help us be capable wives. The beauty of this is that capability is defined by the relevant task. A doctor cannot be called to fly a plane; she is not capable. A mechanic cannot be asked to provide legal advice. You need to spend time in prayer, asking God to make you a capable wife for your husband.

This is the time to ask God to show you things in your heart and past that need to be dealt with as you ask God to make you the wife He has called you to be! This is the time to ask God to help you with the questionable motivations you have identified in your "why," wrong expectations in your "what," and the changes required for your "who"! This is where you lay it all out to God, who can make you the woman He called you to be for the man He is preparing you for!

PREPARE YOUR SOUL

The soul is a bed of the mind, will, and emotions. Without getting into a theological argument on what constitutes the mind versus the spirit, I would like to address that part of us that drives our actions and decisions. I wish I could say it is enough to simply pray and that will guarantee a relationship would materialize. However, evidence in the Bible and our society does not bear this out. Ruth had to go to the threshing floor to ask Boaz to marry her. Rebekah agreed to follow a perfect stranger to become a wife to Isaac. At some point, we need to act on what God is telling us to do as we seek His face during this season of waiting.

We will first deal with our minds, our seat of knowledge and intellect. In preparing for marriage, it is important to learn the right things. The time to learn to swim is not when you are drowning. If you already know how to float before your marriage, you can keep your head above water as you learn new skills in the marriage. Arm yourself with knowledge about marriage before you actually get married.

Next, we will talk about our will! This is about the decisions we make and the things we do. One thing we need to do as single women is get out of our comfort zones. I personally struggle with this, but I am willing to do better than I am doing now. I hope you will as well.

We will then transition to a discussion of our emotions! We are all emotional beings, and the key to waiting with joy lies in keeping our hope alive. I do this by building a Hope Chest, a collection of things that remind me the promise is for an appointed time and though it tarries, it will come to pass.[2]

---

2 Habakkuk 2:3

ARM YOURSELF

At a particular season in my life, I found myself being a guardian to my friend's younger sister. I am the youngest in my nuclear family, so this was a new experience for me. I would tell her, "You are my firstborn, any mistakes I will make with you, I would correct with my children." I learned a lot about myself during this period. I learned I was actually a pushover and not as strict as I thought I was. I learned that I would wake up from a deep sleep with just a single cry from her in the next room. I learned to provide direction without breaking her spirit. I learned to nurse her through sickness. I learned what it meant to be responsible for and manage a household, as opposed to living on my own.

Successful marriages approach this as a lifelong opportunity to study how to dwell in peace with a spouse.

Various things will come as a surprise if we are unprepared for marriage and the responsibilities that come along with it. In this season of waiting, we have the unique opportunity to learn from those who have entered the married state ahead of us. Successful marriages are those that approach marriage as a lifelong opportunity to study how to dwell in peace with a spouse. I am a firm believer there is no time like the present to learn the skills to manage my home. However, if we are not deliberate about learning from others, we will miss out on the opportunity to successfully navigate around avoidable pitfalls.

*"Knowledge is a Weapon, Jon. Arm yourself well
before you ride forth to Battle."*
—George R. R. Martin, *A Dance with Dragons*,
2011

Depending on your circumstances and upbringing,
there will be:

- **Learning to deal with people.** Age does not
  always translate into emotional maturity. This is
  the time to learn how to deal with forgiveness
  and giving of yourself to help others reach their
  goals. This is the time to sponsor a child, get
  an education, or achieve an out of reach dream.
  This is the time to help the single mother in your
  church community, assist the beleaguered mother
  of young children. This is the time to give of
  yourself unselfishly because the truth is, you will
  be able to leave and be all about yourself in a little
  while. Life is nothing if it is all about ourselves.
  We must use our singlehood as freedom to be a
  blessing and not for licentious living

- **Learning to make the right choices.** Being able
  to evaluate decisions and present your reasoning
  process to another human being is a useful skill in
  every facet of life. There are so many jokes about
  how women make decisions with their emotions
  and feelings. What I believe is we have not yet
  learned to put the complex thought processes into
  words that show our decisions are not frivolous.

⅍ Learning to keep a home. Most of us are already managing homes on our own, but what is the tenor of your home. Is it a place where people are happy to come visit, or a beautiful museum? Are you flexible enough to deal with the mess made by children visiting your home? Are you disciplined to keep your home clean enough, so you are not embarrassed when people drop in unannounced? Can you whip up meals to feed your hungry hordes, or at least have some good restaurants on speed dial?

⅍ Learning to manage finances. Some stereotypes for women is we do not know how to manage money appropriately. I have seen women on both sides of the divide, so I can understand the sentiment. However, while some married women can afford to be oblivious to their finances, we cannot do the same. Learn to manage and invest your wealth appropriately like the good steward God made you to be. You never know if you will need to carry on this role after you get married. Part of good financial management is creating a will. A will helps you document your assets and understand what or who you are working for. And no, making a will doesn't mean you are inviting death, any more than going for a check-up means you are inviting illness.

⅍ Learning to be accountable to other people. One of the perks and dangers of being single is you are your own boss. You can drop everything

for a last-minute vacation, spend $400 on a pair
of sunglasses, or spend the entire weekend in
your PJs just because you feel like it. While this
should absolutely be enjoyed, the danger comes
when you have to give up this "freedom" for a
spouse. I have asked a few trusted people to hold
me accountable. Sometimes it is checking to make
sure I am investing in my pension fund. Other
times it is making sure someone knows when I am
taking off. I discuss major life decisions, changing
jobs, moving locations, etc. I do not have to do
this since these are my decisions ultimately, but I
have found it keeps me humble to have to listen
to other people weigh in on my decisions and
challenge my thought process. Ultimately, when
the time comes to get married, I will subject my
choice when dating to respected counselors who
generally can see what I would be blinded to. I am
secure in doing this because I have tested them
with other decisions and developed a trust based
on relationship.

- **Learning to be married.** I love marriage seminars!
I have been attending them faithfully since I was
a teenager, so I think I should be considered a
veteran. One thing that always amazes me is the
people who have been married for fifty years who
still attend faithfully. Speaking to some of these
couples, the constant theme is that there needs
to be a culture of lifelong learning to succeed in
relationships. Attend as many seminars as you can,
read the books, and resolve in your heart that you

will be an eternal student during your marriage. Practice with Jesus, the ultimate Bridegroom while waiting for your knight in shining armor.

GET OUT THERE

- **Do what you love to do**. Spend time doing those things that bring you joy and satisfaction. The best place to meet a soul mate is while doing those things you enjoy. You are likely to be at your best and are confident you will have something in common with the people you meet doing these activities. If you love to run, then join a 5k run. Attending specialized activities like cookery classes and photography for amateurs will not only help you become better at your hobbies, it will provide great avenues to expand your network and meet like-minded people

- **Cultivate new interests.** Now that you have invested in your talents and hobbies, it's time to shake things up a little. Do something out of your comfort zone. Learn a new skill and generally push your boundaries. Sameness leads to boredom while mixing things up refreshes and rejuvenates you as an individual. The sense of accomplishment from succeeding at something different is a confidence booster that helps you lift your head high. This renewed confidence makes you more attractive to others as well, so this is a win-win on

all sides. I am still not willing to go skydiving, but I can probably be convinced to learn Spanish.

ઠ **Volunteer at church.** Be a part of your church community so you can practice what it means to give more than you take. Your local church is a great place to meet new people and develop great relationships. You should not approach this with a predatory mindset, targeting all the single men in the church, but more as an opportunity to associate with people who love God the way you do. I have also found that in a healthy church community, you will have a myriad of opportunities to learn new skills in a risk-free environment.

ઠ **Be friendly.** I frequently remind myself of Proverbs 18:24 that tells me if I will have friends, I must be friendly. I was that child with my nose always stuck in a book, painfully shy in close situations, and extremely uncomfortable with meeting new people. I had to learn that being friendly has never hurt anyone, and a simple smile and willingness to chat goes a long way. I may never be the life of the party, but I can make life a pleasant experience for the next person. I cannot pick and choose who to be friendly to; everyone is worthy of that first chance. Trust me, trying to only be friendly to prospective dates will backfire since you will not always recognize one. Be friendly because God wants you to be an extension of Himself and make the world a better place for the people you come in contact with.

• **Travel if you need to.** Traveling helps expand the breadth of what you are exposed to; different cultures, norms, peoples, and outlook on life. Find a travel buddy and commit to visiting a new place once a year. Travel doesn't need to be expensive to be a wholesome experience. You can drive rather than fly, stay local rather than international, but don't wait to be married before you explore new places. A world out there awaits you with different perspectives and opportunities for growth.

BUILD A HOPE CHEST

I have been trusting God to get married for quite a while now and realized that at various points in my life, I lost hope that this would actually come to pass. I know I have the promise, I know God's Word is faithful and true, but the mere passage of time tends to bring one to where you question whether what God has told you about marriage will still come to pass. As the Bible aptly puts it: *"Unrelenting disappointment leaves you heartsick, but a sudden good break can turn life around"* (Proverbs 13:12 MSG).

One way I dust myself up from heartsickness is to put an item in my hope chest. My hope chest is a collection of items I started gathering for my future husband and home. While I do my best not to hoard stuff I can use currently, I deliberately buy things to remind myself that I will get married and be in a position to use it. In some cases, its lingerie I buy for my honeymoon, perfume I would like to wear on my wedding day, a book for engaged couples I want to study with a currently non-existent fiancé, or even putting money aside to spend for my wedding ceremony. While none of these are set in stone, i.e., I can give them away to people who need them more than I do, I have found the act reminds me I have a hope and it will come to pass.

A hope chest will mean different things to different people and does not have to be a huge financial endeavor. It could be something as cashless as writing letters you intend to give to your spouse. It could be supporting ministries like MarriageToday as an act of faith toward when you are married. Whatever it is should be something that helps you keep hope alive and feeds your faith in the God who is able to make all things beautiful in His time. A word of caution here—this is not to be used as a screen for covetousness, i.e., buying things with a particular person in mind. So long as that man of your dreams is not your fiancé, he is someone else's husband, and buying clothes to fit him counts as covetousness and not faith.

Taking care of our bodies is a responsibility we have, whether that body is joined in marriage to someone else or not.

PREPARE YOUR BODY

You may wonder what it means to prepare your body for marriage. Generally, the points discussed here would apply to us whether we get married or not. Taking care of our bodies is a responsibility we have, whether that body is joined in marriage to someone else or not. Honor God with your body because He gave it to you as a gift!

*You know the old saying, "First you eat to live, and
then you live to eat"? Well, it may be true that the
body is only a temporary thing, but that's no excuse
for stuffing your body with food, or indulging it with
sex. Since the Master honors you with a body, honor
him with your body!* (1 Corinthians 6:13 MSG)

Be beautiful for you. Don't wait until you are in a relationship to take good care of your body. Christ thought
you were worth it and died for you—make His sacrifice
worthwhile.

WATCH WHERE YOU SLEEP

Respect your body enough not to have sex outside of marriage. Our society right now is at the point where this is no
longer clearly defined in the church. Cohabitation and hook-
ing up have become so ingrained in society that the church
has been infected with it. Without mincing words or assuming you know this already, do not have sex with someone
who has not had the courage or inclination to marry you.

Don't buy into the lie that other women are not waiting for marriage so why should you? There are many virgins
and sexually abstinent women out there who are paying
the price to wait. Everyone is not sleeping around! It has,
unfortunately, become a thing of ridicule to remain a virgin
until marriage, but for the sake of the younger generation,
this needs to change. If you have been blessed enough to
remain a virgin, then lift up your head and be bold about it.
Let the world know, "I am a Christian. I choose to abstain

from sex until I am within the confines of marriage." This is not to rub it into the noses of those who have been sexually intimate in the past. Old things have passed away, and in the eyes of God, you are a virgin too! If you are still sexually intimate, you can stop today.

It may seem like a tough decision, but I can assure you that if you found out today your boyfriend had HIV, you would develop the willpower to say no to him immediately. Let the fear of sinning against God do that to you as well. Run from sin the same way you would run to preserve your life. It doesn't matter how many times you fall, what matters is that you get back up again. God has called both male and female to a higher standard of righteousness, and we need to live our lives to please Him.

If you have gone through abuse—know this: It is not your fault. You did not do anything to deserve it! If you find yourself in a self-destructing cycle of addictive behavior to deal with the pain, you need to get some help. Find a good Christian counselor who can help you and pray with you as God heals you from the pain of your past.

WATCH WHAT YOU EAT

Respect your body enough to watch what and when you eat. This is a touchy one for us girls since we care so much about how we look. I do not intend to go into the pros and cons of weight loss programs, but I would like to encourage you to eat healthily, so you can be healthy.

One of the first steps is to stop complaining about the way you look. If you can do something about your weight, then by all means, go ahead. I have met a good number of people who gained weight from medication and health challenges, and it is tough to get rid of it. However, everyone can benefit from eating right, even if it doesn't lead to changes in your weight. In the end, you need to love yourself the way God loves you—unconditionally! If you do not learn to accept yourself the way you are, you will constantly be trying to change something just to be accepted. God loves you just the way you are, and gaining or losing weight is not going to change His opinion of you one little bit.

I constantly marvel at the reactions I get about my weight from other people. I have gone from being a skinny Size 0 to a Size 4 over a period of ten years. Depending on when people have met me, I get a "You are so fat now" to a "You are so tiny." I really don't know who to believe, but I realize my self-esteem cannot be based on my weight.

I will simply tell you that we are all so different and what weight program works for someone else may not necessarily work for you. Sometimes it's not your quantities that are off but your timing. Conventional wisdom says to eat a good breakfast, a heavy lunch, and a light supper before 8 PM. For me, this was the key to losing stubborn weight—simply a decision not to eat past a certain time.

WATCH WHAT YOU DO

We have a responsibility to give our bodies the best shot at longevity that we can. Some of that comes through regular exercise to keep those joints healthy. I am not a big fan of jumping jacks, so simple things like taking the stairs or walking short distances rather than driving go a long way for me. If your job is sedentary, you need to go out of your way to make sure you move. Don't let people wait on you hand and foot—get up and take the water out of the fridge yourself! Owning a Fitbit showed me how sedentary I had become and helped me improve over time.

In addition to exercising, it is also vital to get adequate sleep and be kind to your body. You have only one body to use in this life—use it wisely!

WATCH HOW IT WORKS

Work regular check-ups with doctors into your routine. For forgetful people like me, you can tie it to your birth month, so you always remember when you last had a check-up. Breast exams should be done with increasing regularity as you grow older. Remember, there's no husband right now to accidentally discover the lump on your behalf. Also, make sure you are taking vitamins regularly and following the doctors' orders for your particular situation.

Watch out for red flags from your family history and diligently work toward a healthier you. A school of thought says you shouldn't go through life worried about the ailments that have plagued your family since you are now a Christian. I believe a lot of this is simply burying your head in the sand because we do not want to face tough things. Based on my family history, I check my cholesterol regularly and watch certain foods I eat. I am not walking in fear of having a heart attack but cooperating with God to keep my body healthy. I can now pray specifically, "God, keep my cholesterol down," which is an even more specific expression of what I am asking God for.

WATCH HOW IT LOOKS

In my fourth year in college, I was praying one morning when I heard God ask me, "Why don't you use makeup every day?" It took some soul searching, but I finally told God what He was waiting to hear, it was all due to fear. Let me explain. I had seen the transformation makeup brought to my features and the resulting double looks from male friends who used to be "safe." I could not stand the pain of a friend developing a romantic interest and then losing that friendship if the "romance" did not work out.

I discovered that morning that my refusal to wear makeup was more about protecting my heart than not having time to put it on every morning. I got up from my bed and told a friend to keep me accountable, so I would obey what God was dealing with me about. The point of the story is not to tell you to wear makeup if you don't want to. Instead, I am trying to get you to understand that God cares about something as simple as that and your reasons behind not wearing them. Now I wear light makeup every day and suffer through makeovers from my friends for special occasions. I have learned to embrace the beauty in the face God has given me and have given my fear over to Him. I want to encourage you to go through life putting your best face forward. Be comfortable with what "you" look like and look beautiful in the way you dress and look!

Do it for your first husband, i.e., God—who longs to see you dressed up for Him! He made you beautiful; He made you you! Don't hide your beauty behind a bushel—let it shine!

IN CONCLUSION

> *Don't hide your beauty behind a bushel—let it shine!*

Over the past few chapters, we have dealt with the strategy of waiting for marriage. We examined our motivations, our expectations, our responsibilities, and in this chapter our actions as we eagerly anticipate getting married at a future date. Waiting becomes easier when we understand what we need to be consumed with during that period. I encourage you to go over these chapters again and develop your personal strategy for how you will approach facets of your life going forward.

LIFE APPLICATION

1. Do you believe God wants you to get married?

2. Do you have a habit of praying for your future spouse? What are the reasons you may or may not do this?

3. What avenues do you currently use to prepare yourself for marriage? Are there any new things you will explore?

4. Do you have a hope chest? Share ideas of things you would put in there. What other methods do you use to keep yourself in hope?

5. How do you feel about your body? What changes do you need to make to take good care of your body in the future?

Wait—Now What!

I think one of the most tragic Bible stories is of Michal, the daughter of Saul. She fell in love with David, and eventually, became his first wife after he killed one hundred Philistines for the privilege. Here she was, the daughter of the first king of Israel, married to the man widely rumored to be her father's successor. When political intrigue struck, she sided with her husband against her father and helped David escape the plot against his life.

I imagine she waited for David to send for her since she had proven her love, but during all his years in exile, he never did; she had been forgotten. She heard the news his parents had joined him, then his brothers, yet no Michal. He took a new wife and then another, but she was not sent for. Then came the day her father gave her away in marriage to another man, figuring David had deserted her. This man loved her and took care of her, and I would like to believe she would have been happy with him.

But politics struck again, and she was taken away from him as a condition for peace between her father's house and David's. The Bible records her husband followed her, weeping uncontrollably from a distance until he was forced to go back. She might have consoled herself that she could find love again with David, but where she was his only wife when she first met him, now she was one of seven. While he was a shepherd cum warrior in the beginning, he was now a king. Her dreams met up with reality and were found wanting. I imagine she was disappointed and sad, then angry and bitter at the way her life had turned out. In the end, she treated David with contempt, and we are told she remained childless until her death.

> *I ask you now to run a health check on your heart and mind! Are you heart healthy? Is your mind sound?*

Michal didn't get to this point in one day. She harbored her pain and resentment until it simmered out into disrespect for the king and for God. Though she got the raw end of the deal from David, she put herself in a position where God would not fight for her! She had let the little foxes spoil her vines!

I ask you now to run a health check on your heart and mind! Are you heart healthy? Is your mind sound?

GUARD YOUR HEART

> *"Keep vigilant watch over your heart; that's where life starts"* (Proverbs 4:23 MSG).

I figure if God asks us to watch the heart diligently, it must take very little to get it corrupted. We have a duty to guard, i.e., place restrictions and parameters around our hearts to

keep it safe. A polluted heart affects our lives in more ways than one.

One way to see if your heart is healthy is noting how you react to good news from others. Are your friends able to share success and challenges without having to filter the details for fear of offending you? Does every story about something great that happened in someone's life end with the statement, Why doesn't anything good happen to me? I get that you will still be amazed when your twice-divorced friend announces she is getting married again. My question to you is, are you able to set aside your feelings and longings for the same—to rejoice with the person who has the good news now? Will you receive the news of your friends' courtship with the outlook that God can do the same thing for you?

It is a constant struggle to keep our hearts pure, so don't ignore the hurt or jealousy that tries to pop up. I find it helps me to tell God about it and set out to bless the happy couple any way I can. It could be gifts, time, or praying for them, but I choose to act outside my feelings, so I can keep my heart healthy.

A few things we need to guard our hearts against are:

- **Disappointment**—"Hope deferred makes the heart sick; but when dreams come true at last, there is life and joy" (Proverbs 13:12–14 TLB).

    Stay expectant that you will get married. It's difficult to keep hope alive when year after year, failed relationship after failed relationship occurs. Give the disappointment to God and keep your heart healthy by faith. Remind yourself what God has said to you and ask Him to lift up your spirit. I tell God, hope deferred is making my heart sick, please heal my heart and keep it healthy. You know what, He always does. He sends something or someone to encourage me, who picks me up when I am down! The key here is not to hide the hurt from God, instead, give it to Him to take it away.

֍ **Bitterness**—Don't allow bitterness to set in your heart. Bitterness is birthed from unresolved anger, which ultimately means we are holding back forgiveness from someone.

Bitterness comes up when you believe you have gotten the wrong end of the stick. The truth is you may have! Someone may have cheated on you and caused you pain. Or you may have followed the rules all your life and served God faithfully, and it looks like there is nothing to show for it. Bitterness causes you to lash out at other people as it consumes you and robs you of rational behavior. It causes more hurt to you than to the other person, and will always drive people away from you in the end. You need to let it go for your emotional health, not because someone asks for it or deserves it.

֍ **Emotional Attachments**—It's really easy to form emotional attachments to guys who are nice to us, even when we know they are not right for us. Apart from the obvious, married men, criminals, and abusive men; we need to be on our guard to avoid giving our hearts to someone who hasn't asked for it. If a guy doesn't desire you enough to give voice to the vibes he is sending, call him out on it. Make sure you don't start planning the wedding when he is only trying to be nice to you. Heed these words that appear three times in the Songs of Solomon, "*Young women of Jerusalem, swear to me by the gazelles or by the does in the field that you will not awaken love or arouse love before its proper time.*" (Songs of Solomon 3:5, God's Word (GW))

If you have already formed these attachments, you need to break them off now. Most times we need some help and accountability to get out of this, so ask for help if you need it. Contrary to public opinion, you will not die of a broken heart! God, not time, will heal all wounds and restore your heart to a place of health and joy as you stay open to him!

RENEW YOUR MIND

I get it you say. I understand I have some things I need to change about how I think or see life. What do I do to change these destructive mindsets? How do I renew my mind? I believe identifying the issue is half the battle. Subsequently, train your mind with what you say, read, and do to value the new mindset. Notice I said train, denoting a repetitive action that keeps reinforcing the good and punishing the bad behavior. It means talking aloud to yourself when you have negative thoughts. It's making yourself go visit someone you would not normally associate with due to unfounded prejudices. It involves asking God to change your heart to where you can love the way He loves, to see people the way He sees them. It is taking firm action to fight a battle for your mind, and this will not change without thoughtful and deliberate action. The good news is, this is a battle that can be won!

> *"Don't copy the behavior and customs of this world, but let God transform you into a new person by changing the way you think. Then you will learn to know God's will for you, which is good and pleasing and perfect"* (Romans 12:2 NLT).

Some unhealthy things we need to identify and work through in our minds are Inner vows, Fear, and Hurt.

a) **Inner Vows**

I learned about the concept of inner vows from Jimmy Evans[1], a marriage and relationship teacher based in Texas. He explained this as a self-directed promise resulting from difficulty or pain. We typically make these vows to ourselves when we are much younger with statements like, "I'll never . . .," "I'll always . . .," or "When I grow

---

1   MarriageToday

up . . .," etc. The problem with inner vows is
they manifest a behavior that defies reasoning,
i.e., not a direct response to the stimulus on the
ground. After I lost my dad, I went from having
almost all my clothes from the UK to using a
local tailor for most of my clothes. I remember
telling myself, "When I grow up, I will buy as
many ready-made clothes as I like."

You may have seen your dad being stingy
with money with your mom and vowed, No
man will ever have control over my finances.
Your mom may have been "too submissive,"
and you decide never to submit to any man. It
could be you were poor growing up and vowed
never to deny yourself anything you want.

These vows are responses to incidents in
our past that make us wary and unreasonable
to similar circumstances in the future. It
is clear that a decision never to allow your
husband to have a say in your finances will
generate issues in your future. Inner vows need
to be dealt with as they are discovered. I have
to remind myself every time I am tempted
to buy new clothes that I am not that child
anymore. I have learned to walk into a store
and walk out without purchasing a thing. I am
practicing for when my husband and I are on a
budget, so we can buy a new house or prepare
for a new child. I am telling myself that
submission to my husband is a sign of strength
not weakness.

b) **Fear**

Fear, as they say, is a self-fulfilling prophecy. A constant focus on your fears would either paralyze you when it comes to making the right decisions or cause you to make an incorrect choice. There are different fears we face as single women:

- Fear that you won't get married.

- Fear that you will make a wrong choice.

- Fear that this person hovering around you now may be your last chance.

- Fear that God will bring someone you don't like your way.

- Fear that the person God is opening your eyes to see is not up to snuff.

- Fear that by the time God does it, you would have lost time.

- Fear that you will not be able to recover all you have lost from the delay when you eventually get married.

- Fear that you are praying about the wrong things for your future spouse.

- Fear that when you said no to a prior suitor, you missed God's plan for you.

ᴥ Fear that you will fail in marriage when you
   eventually get married.

ᴥ Fear that you will no longer be able to have
   children when you get married.

Sweeping your fears under the carpet will
not resolve the issues, but acknowledging these
fears and building up your faith to combat
them will. When my fears rear their ugly head,
I speak to myself; *I will not miss it, I will hear
a voice behind me saying this is the way, walk
in it. The plans God has for me are to give me a
future and a hope. My times are in God's hands.*
Give your fears over to God and trust that He
has your best interests at heart. In addition to
fighting your fears with faith, it helps to reason
them through to the end. I always ask myself,
what is the worst that can happen? Doing this
helps me identify what I need to work on to
combat that particular fear.

In many cases, you can take practical
steps to change the outcome you fear. If you
are afraid of drowning, you can learn how to
swim. If you fear failure, study the principles
others used to be successful. Fear of failure
in marriage should drive you to marriage
seminars and "internships" with happily
married couples.

Fear that is not dealt with will become a
cancer in your life, causing you to do irrational

things. Take some time today to catalog and deal with your fears with God's help! He has not given us a spirit of fear but of love, of power, and of a sound mind!

c) **Hurt**

Sometimes it's hard to move past hurt, and this hinders us from moving forward. Holding on to past hurts is like running backward. Progress is slow, and the entire endeavor is dangerous. Hurt can come from past emotional or physical abuse. It could be from the pain of a broken relationship or betrayed trust. It may be the death of a boyfriend or fiancé. To be honest about it, there are heartbreaking stories out there and legitimate reasons to hold on to hurt for an extended period of time.

I remember going through a broken relationship and for the first time finding myself unable to snap out of the pain I was feeling. I was constantly frustrated by well-meaning friends who would tell me to just snap out of it. I always wondered how I was supposed to do this. Give me practical things to do that will help me to get out of this funk I find myself in. I don't think you can put grief or healing on a timer. Everyone heals at their own pace. I will, however, share some tips that helped me to get beyond a world of hurt and regain my cheerful outlook on life.

❧ **Take it one day at a time.** The sun will rise the next morning. The world has not stopped because of my pain. There is a joy ahead, a peace to strive for in the future. Today may seem like the worst day of my life, but there will be a tomorrow, and it will be better than my today. The constancy of life helped ground me and show me the world did not end with the hurt I encountered.

❧ **Acknowledge the pain.** It's okay to mourn the loss or circumstances causing your pain. The key is to get up from that place of pain and rejoin life. I was in a meeting at work for women, and one facilitator talked about a rule her husband instituted in their home. His rule was that every failure or success was agonized over or raved about for the next twenty-four hours. Then, at the end of that period, it became another event in history, another unpleasant memory or success to be built on. I really connected with this idea because it allowed me the time to hurt without wallowing in it. Use your own version of the twenty-four-hour rule to deal with your hurts. Weep, cry, scream, but realize you have a time limit to really mourn before you have to face the next day; one step at a time.

❧ **Learn the right things from the experience.** It's amazing how different people face similar issues and learn different things. I remember a friend's mom telling me how she effortlessly snapped back to her pre-pregnancy weight after the first four children. After having the fifth child, she started a battle with weight gain that she still struggled with ten years later. After this, she paused and asked me what I had learned from her story. Tongue in cheek, I responded, stop after four children!

> *Don't give your past the right to destroy your future.*

I say that to illustrate how we can leave an experience without learning the right lesson. A woman who has fallen prey to a deceitful man will either learn to recognize deceit more easily or decide all men are deceitful. A woman who has lost her fiancé may decide never to put her heart at risk again or be grateful for the time she had with her departed love. Choose what you will learn from what hurts you! If you have already learned the wrong things, take some time to unlearn them. Don't give your past the right to destroy your future. Stop the cycle of hurt with the healing that only God provides.

❧ Share your pain with people who can help.
Someone once said "A burden shared is a burden lifted." This truth is probably better stated in Galatians 6:2 "Share each other's burdens, and in this way obey the law of Christ" (NLT). Talking through hurt with a wise counselor lightens the pain. Just talking about it helps combat the near sainthood status we tend to apply to people who have left. Talking helps point out troubling

patterns in our thought processes and just helps
people know how to be there through the pain.
While I acknowledge there are people who would
make it worse, keep searching until you find a
safe place. You don't have to look any further than
God! He can take your pain and insecurities. He
is not threatened when you challenge Him or are
angry you have to go through pain. Whatever you
do, don't close the channel of communication;
both to God and to your close confidantes.

&➤ **Don't be afraid to seek help.** Sometimes you just
need more help than you can get from your friends
and family. If you have fallen into depression, see
a doctor. If there are deep-rooted issues of abuse,
visit a qualified Christian counselor, pastor, or
psychologist. If suicidal thoughts are pervasive,
please reach out to someone to get help. There is
no shame in needing a helping hand. Anyone who
makes you feel that way has not been through
enough in life. God has provided a way of help
because He knew in this fallen world, we would
not always be able to hear His voice reaching
out to us. Reach out for help rather than suffer a
mental breakdown from grief.

DEVELOP THE RIGHT ATTITUDE

One of the most popular parables in the Bible is the Prodigal Son. Growing up, I thought it referred to the fact the

younger son went away, and it took a few years to realize he was wasteful. But as much as the story is about the younger brother, I tend to relate more to the older brother.

I could never understand why the father did not immediately throw a party for the older son to encourage him not to leave like his younger brother. Why didn't the father give him more servants to wait on him hand and foot in reward for his steadfastness?

Why wasn't the older brother consulted on the wisdom of taking back the younger brother, or the position he would now occupy in the household on his return? After all, the possessions left were all the older brother's share of the inheritance; so it stands to reason he should have a say in how it was spent on charity.

> *The older brother became angry and refused to go in. So his father went out and pleaded with him. But he answered his father, "Look! All these years I've been slaving for you and never disobeyed your orders. Yet you never gave me even a young goat so I could cel-ebrate with my friends. But when this son of yours who has squandered your property with prostitutes comes home, you kill the fattened calf for him!" (Luke 15:28–30)*

I felt he was justified in his anger, and I could relate to some of his complaints in my walk with God. I joined Him to say, "God, I have been living for You. I do my best not to disobey You, yet You haven't given me what I have been asking You for. When will it be my turn to celebrate and be celebrated? I believe I deserve to be blessed because I have

not strayed from Your way. Why then do you bless the wayward but repentant woman before steadfast little old me?"

The Father's response baffles me to this day.

> *"My son," the father said, "you are always with me,*
> *and everything I have is yours. But we had to cel-*
> *ebrate and be glad, because this brother of yours was*
> *dead and is alive again; he was lost and is found."*
> (Luke 15:31–32)

YOU ARE ALWAYS WITH ME! This is a love relationship. You already have everything I have!

While I had been focusing on what I was doing for
God, He was focusing on the relationship He has with me.
While I was looking for possessions and gifts to prove God
loves me, He was establishing my position as His firstborn
and heir to all He possessed. While I was offended by His
rejoicing over a wayward child, He was showing me that I
should be secure in the unconditional love He displays to
all who would come to Him. Every day is a blessing from
God; every blessing is a gift from God.

To the outside world, the older brother was doing
everything right, but the arrival of the younger brother
revealed the wrong attitude in his heart.

I learned a lot from the older brother in this parable.
I don't want to give everyone the impression I am content
in my singleness if I am harboring resentment because God
gave a "prodigal" sister a husband before mine showed up.

I learned I need to take my eyes off myself and what I
am "doing" for God.

I chose to keep my eyes on Jesus, on the ultimate relationship that means the world to me.

I learned I could be joyful even before I see my dreams come to pass.

I learned to keep things in perspective. The world does not revolve around me. Someone else getting blessed is not a reflection on me, it's a blessing for them!

I learned to be joyful in hope, patient in affliction, and faithful in prayer[2].

I learned that godliness with contentment is great gain[3]

I learned to be thankful in all things[4]

I learned I can face life with the right attitude; not entitled, but grateful for what I have in hand and what I have in hope.

> *I learned I can face life with the right attitude; not entitled, but grateful for what I have in hand and what I have in hope.*

IN CONCLUSION

Keeping our hearts and minds healthy is essential to help us avoid self-inflicted delay and pain. Getting rid of the heart and mind issues also opens our mind to be able to see, hear, and do what God is speaking to us clearly. We can then face the future with an attitude of faith, hope, and love, knowing the time of waiting is not forever.

---

2 Romans 12:12 (NIV)

3 1 Timothy 6:6 (NIV)

4 1 Thessalonians 5:18

LIFE APPLICATION

1. What was your response to the question—Is your heart healthy, is your mind sound? What are the things you have identified in your heart and mind that you need to deal with?

2. Do you have anything you have identified as an inner vow that you need to deal with?

3. Write down any fears you may currently have about relationships. What is the worst that can happen if that fear is realized? What can you do about it?

4. Have you had to overcome any emotional attachments? How did you get over this?

5. Do you have any trusted counselors you can talk with when you have issues or concerns?

10

Wait—You're Not Helping!

When the idea for this book first came to me, one thing I knew I needed to include was a chapter for family, friends, and the church on dealing with single women. This was because of the many tales of insensitive statements I have listened to over the years that have caused hurt to single women. I have given many hugs and helped wipe away countless tears as a result of well-intentioned conversations gone awry. I have realized that many people simply do not know how to deal with the older single women they know and love. It is not an attempt to be cruel so much as a lack of knowledge on what is taboo and what is kosher.

So these next few words are for you, dear family member, friend, or fellow believer. I want to believe your desire is not just to see us married, but to see us marry well. The truth is, this is our desire as well, so we should ideally be working toward the same goal. I don't know if your prior comments or actions have driven a wedge between you and your loved one. I applaud the fact you want to do better going forward, and I pray this perspective will help you work on restoring and maintaining your relationship going forward.

FAMILY

I think that a good family is probably the most important stabilizing factor for single women. I recently lost a friend to breast cancer and what struck me through her hospital and eventually hospice stay was the support from her family. Her family sacrificed time, income, traveled long distances and bent over backward to make her last days memorable. Someone would say that this should be the case even if she had been married. Unfortunately, too many of us single women end up distant from family as a result of offenses taken over not being married.

I know that as family, you want the best for your daughter or sister, and in most cases, that best involves having her settled down in a home. My mother would always remark that no matter how bad a mother's experience is in marriage, she still wants her daughter to get married. Maybe it's to be able to welcome grandchildren or to keep wagging tongues at bay. Whatever the reasons, the pressure that comes from the family can be a tremendous source of heartache to a single woman.

In case you are reading this book and have unmarried women around you, I would like you to read this letter written on behalf of many single women everywhere. I know you may not agree with everything in this letter. In fact, I would be surprised if every part of this letter relates entirely to you. There will be parts you can ignore and in some others you will have valid reasons to justify some of your prior actions. I simply ask you to keep an open mind and see things from our perspective. I ask you to see us as individuals and not our marital status.

Dear Family,

I want to start by thanking you for being an amazing family. I am blessed to be able to call you kin! I know that not everyone has the opportunity to belong to a family that cares about their welfare. Rest assured, I do not take your love and concern for granted. I want to be able to come home to family events and pick up the phone without hesitation.

This is why I feel the need to air some of my concerns to you now, in the hope we can come to an understanding that benefits us all. I would like to speak plainly about some things that have become a source of friction between us. Please understand, my intention is not to offend, and I apologize in advance if my words do just that.

I am single! This is not a curse or disease. It is simply a fact that I am not married at the moment. I know you want me to get married, but I would like to think you do not simply want me married, you want me happily married. Unfortunately, sometimes it seems as if getting me married is more about fulfilling your accomplishment or getting people off your back. Please realize, you are not the one who is alone at night and during the holidays.

I am more than a marital status. Please see me beyond someone who is not married. While I know you should ask about what is going on in the relationship department, you should be interested in other aspects of my life as well. Be happy for me when I am promoted, buy a new house, or learn a new language. These should be causes of celebration whether I am married or not. Don't diminish my joy because one part of my life is not all I want it to be. I ask you to rejoice with me over accomplishments, even when they are not marital because as you know, the world does not end after one gets married.

I would like you to respect my privacy. Right now, I am my own family unit, so be careful not to barge into my private space uninvited. My life is not an open book for public discussion on the subject of marriage. I see the respect you give my married siblings in matters concerning their home and wonder why I do not deserve the same consideration. Understand that I may choose to remain single and respect my decisions, even if you do not agree with them.

Do not take this to mean I am pushing you away. I need you to ask how I am doing. I need you to be interested in how I am doing as a person. By all means, check up on me around special holidays. Yes, make time to talk to me since I don't have a spouse to confide in. I am simply asking you to look beyond the outward to the person beneath.

Sometimes I need you to protect me from the "good intentioned interventions" of the broader family. I may not always be able to fight for myself, but you can fight for me. While in the middle of family dinners, I do not respond well to twenty people asking me when I am going to get married. Staging an intervention to discuss my unmarried state is as insensitive as probing the reason for a lack of children in another person's home. I will do my best to be gracious since not everyone is under your control. Please realize continued harping on being single will drive me away out of necessity so I can keep my heart healthy.

I know you feel the need to do something to help me get married. You may think I need help meeting new people, so you go out of your way to set me up on blind dates. Will you please let me know when there will be company, so I am not blindsided? Let's make a deal—if you promise not to push, I promise to be courteous. Your role in this is to facilitate, not enforce. Assuming I must connect with every prospective suitor you bring my way is erroneous.

When the time comes that I give you access to comment on potential suitors, please use that privilege wisely. This is not the time to shove your opinions or preferences on race, color, or pedigree down my throat. I am letting you in because you can see things in my relationships that I may be blind to. I commit to keeping myself open to your observations, but I want to be able to trust they are not from your personal biases but are valid concerns. Don't gloss over bad behavior or red flags in my dates just because I haven't dated in a while. Be the voice of reason for me and don't pressure me to settle for less than God's best. Take time to ask God for the wisdom required to present your concerns in a manner I can receive it. Be empathetic, especially when discussing red flags. I do not want to become bitter and hide relationships from you in the future.

Please pray for me, not at me; and not as if there is no plight worse than not being married. I know God has good plans for me—plans to give me a future and a hope. Whether that involves marriage or not, time will tell. I have made up my mind to live for Him regardless.

I am thankful for the support system you provide and do not take this for granted. I would not be the woman I am today if I did not have you in my life.

Thank you for being an amazing family.

Love Always,

FRIENDS

I have a good friend who got married in her late thirties. After some delay in having children, she ended up with two children under the age of two and had to juggle caring for them with a demanding career. We were catching up on life, and she made a statement that struck me. "Now I can also say I am busy." You see, during the time she was single, she was told this statement by people she considered friends as an explanation for why they didn't stay in touch. "I am busy" became a goal for her to attain. It was her way of dealing with the pain of being forgotten by friends dear to her.

The issue is not really being busy. After all, true friendship requires us to lend a helping hand to an overwhelmed mother. Sometimes what you hear is the subtle statement behind it like "you are not married and have no kids, so you do not understand what it means to be busy. You are not married so you should not be putting on weight. You are not married so you cannot afford to lose your hair. You are not married, so you are always available." Marriage seems to be the foil for things unacceptable for singles.

These sometimes snide and often insensitive remarks are a form of disrespect singles deal with on a regular basis. As a friend, please work hard to make sure this is not coming from you as well.

Be sensitive to single people around you. Call them on birthdays and holidays as this is when we are the most vulnerable. Look for singles around you who do not seem to have family close by and open your home to them. Be the friend that sticks closer than a brother!

"Do not forsake your friend or a friend of your family, and do not go to your relative's house when disaster strikes you—better a neighbor nearby than a relative far away" (Proverbs 27:10).

THREE IS A CROWD

In my last year in college, I went to a dinner with a group of friends and realized I was the only one unattached. Seven of us arrived at the dinner, but the tables were only arranged to seat six. I remember going to another table and sitting with people I had never met, wondering throughout the dinner why I was still there. I learned a valuable lesson that day, and that was to look out for people around me. I never told my friends how I felt, as I knew they were not trying to be mean. It's human nature to be involved with someone and not notice when other people are being left out. I believe it is possible to make an effort to involve singles around us without making them feel like a third wheel. It's okay to continue with your PDAs, but prolonged exposure to this is tantamount to saying to someone, "go home so we can get on with it."

The days of chatting through the night may be over, but planning a special time, however infrequent, assures us that we still matter to you.

On my part, I want to be involved in the lives of my married friends. But I do not want to spend all our time together talking about your husband and the cute things your kids did. Friendship is give and take—I care about what you care about, and I want you to feel the same way toward me and what I care about.

SINGLE IS NOT SPELLED J E Z E B E L

Have you been in situations where married women don't want you around their husbands because they think you might be having designs on them? I am talking about the cloak of suspicion often cast on innocent women who are suspected of trying to wreck homes and replace the current wife. I am fully aware there are many such women out there who would stop at nothing to displace the wife in the home. By all means, protect your home from these women by every means possible. While you are doing this though, please remember some of us are just looking to be friends with people our age. I tend to give my close male friends a wide berth once they get married, as I want to ensure their wife is comfortable with our friendship. I have lost a few in the long run, but what I have gained most times is a new friend in the wife and a good relationship with the kids, while maintaining a good relationship with the husband. I have learned to reach out to the wife, or husband as the case may be, then accept my relationship has to be modified for it to continue and be willing to let go if there is friction. God will bring other friends to replace the ones I let go for the good of their family.

CHURCH

When looking from the outside in, marriage seems to be the preferred state in the church. I imagine this is due to Paul's advice to Timothy, asking him to ensure the deacon and the pastor is the husband of one wife. In many circles, this has disqualified single people from positions of authority. Some denominations do not believe in ordaining women, which places a double whammy on single women. I personally believe it shouldn't matter if you have a position, so long as you are doing what God wants you to do.

Marriage is not superior to singleness. Singleness is not superior to marriage!

Because I believe this, I ask God to change my heart, and I work to renew my mind when I see single women passed over because they are not married. I also see women in positions of authority in the church who are only there because of who they are married to. There needs to be time and effort poured into helping these women grow into the responsibility thrown on them by marriage. Oftentimes, the single woman in a church leadership position has already proven herself elsewhere before she is appointed a leader in the church. I think we all agree the church is not the place for ambition or striving for position, nor should it be a popularity contest. This is not a church bashing session. In my personal experience, I have been blessed to belong to churches that invest in the women who worship there. The point of this discussion is to mention that Paul placed singleness at the same level of importance as marriage (maybe higher). Let's watch the subtle ways we as Christians portray things differently. Marriage is not superior to singleness. Single-ness is not superior to marriage!

> *"Sometimes I wish everyone were single like me—a simpler life in many ways! But celibacy is not for everyone any more than marriage is. God gives the gift of the single life to some, the gift of the married life to others"* (1 Corinthians 7:7 MSG).

THE GRASS IS GREEN

I remember attending a marriage seminar when I was a teenager and being bothered by one example shared at the event. The speaker told the story of a highly educated woman who was still single and asking God to provide her a husband. She would eventually marry her gardener, ostensibly at God's instruction.

This bothered me because the speaker took an unusual circumstance and taught it as a principle. There was no caveat about the challenges that could arise because the couple may not have common ground to talk about. There was no view or follow up to the quality of the marriage after a few years. I have met women who married men with lower educational qualifications. I even have a friend who married someone who was illiterate at the time she married him. In every one of these circumstances, they were intel-lectually compatible even when their formal education did not match up. My issue was the speaker's "testimony" had the flavor of a fairy tale—the result without the process. What these types of stories have led to is a generation of women nursing fears about letting God lead them concerning marriage. So my appeal is to you fellow Christian—tell the truth about marriage.

If I had a penny for every time I heard "When I was single," I would be quite wealthy by now. There is always a married woman who tells you not to rush into marriage because of the many challenges. What rings hollow is the lack of discussion on the joys of marriage, probably to prevent single women from becoming despondent about not being married.

What ends up happening is a lack of connection with the women you hope to encourage. After all, you are going home to your husband and children. You do not have to hug a pillow at night since you hopefully have your support system in place. Watching happily married couples is not a threat to the single woman. It is something to look forward to, a representation of the love we desire. So share your joy as well as your pain. This is what rings true. Tell the good, the bad and the ugly. There are joys and pain in marriage just like there are joys and pain in singlehood. The grass is green on both sides—not greener!

IT'S NOT MY FAULT

One of the harder things for singles to forgive is when someone turns around and blames them for not being married. I can empathize with the preacher who has been praying and declares, "By this time next year, you will be in your husband's house." What I cannot comprehend is how I am now the one to blame when you come back next year and,

I am still single. I have heard pastors say that God always backs up their words with a performance of the word and thus if I do not see the manifestation, it is because there is sin or unbelief in my life. Frankly, I have enough to deal with without someone dumping the responsibility of their unanswered prayers on me.

The truth is, I have wanted to be a millionaire for a long time. I have been in services where the anointing to make people millionaires was prayed over us. Yet, I have never heard someone go to the pastor and say the reason you are not a millionaire is there is sin or unbelief in your life. In the church, we have this deep-rooted desire to be able to explain things on God's behalf until everything fits together in a neat little package with a tidy bow. This existed in the time of Jesus when His disciples sought to understand why a man was blind from birth; He taught them it is not always someone's fault that things are the way they are in their life.

I guess my message is simple—thank you for praying for me, thank you for staying in touch with me. Yes, I am single, but no, you do not need to find a reason for why that is. It is a season of my life, and I intend to make the best of it—guilt free!

HOLD MY HAND UP

I was invited to speak at one session at a women's conference a few years ago, and I shared a message about being single, saved, and satisfied. I remember one thing I spoke about was that during women's conferences, single women (and I guess women still trying to get pregnant) are often at a loss for what to do when the subject turns to praying for your children. I encouraged them to put their hands on their stomach and pray for that child who has not yet physically manifested.

Fast forward—two to three sessions later, as predicted, we were being led to pray for our children! One would think I would jump in and practice what I had just preached, but I was emotionally spent and just sat there with my head in my hands. Just then, one woman I traveled to the conference with took my hand and placed it on my stomach. That simple gesture broke through the pain, disappointment, and frustration of that moment. Every time I remember this incident, tears well up in my eyes as I recall how she literally held up my arms as Aaron and Hur did for Moses. I tell this story because there will be multiple times when some single lady around you will grow tired, and her hands will hang down. Be sensitive to the need around you and lift up those weary hands. It's not always in words; it's never an act of pity—it's a sign of solidarity, a token to say we are in this time together and I am here when you need me.

MY OWN COMPANY

A few years ago, my friend and I moved to a new city and joined a church which did not have a singles fellowship. Since we thought this was a crucial need considering the number of young people in the church, we got leadership approval to survey the congregation and help design a program that would fit the demographic.

During this process, a lady in her forties approached me to discuss what we intended to do. After giving her the lowdown on what the vision was shaping up to be, she looked me in the eye and asked, "What about me?"

In sending out the survey, we screened out the older singles, the single mothers, the divorcees, and the widows. We essentially said to them, there is no place for you here. You have outgrown the age bracket for our singles definition. In old English jargon, you are firmly on the shelf. We went back to the drawing board to see if there was anything we could do to cater to the older, single crowd. Sadly, we did not have the resources to tackle that need at that time.

Now that I am the older single woman, I more fully appreciate what this dear lady was pointing out to me.

The women's fellowship in many churches needs to be renamed the married women's fellowship as they cater mostly to this focus group. Mature singles find most of their age-mates in the women's fellowship, but the content can be so focused on marriage that it is uncomfortable for singles, divorced, and single moms. Most singles' fellowships cater to people in their twenties, making the older ladies instant coordinators or mother figures. Given the traditional divisions of specialized fellowships, it has become very easy to completely overlook this fast-growing segment of the congregation.

I ask you to evaluate your specialized fellowships and ensure you have a place that welcomes all categories. If you discover you have a large enough group to meet, then start a fellowship for these groups. You may be surprised at the number of guests you will have from neighboring churches who are simply looking for some fellowship with their own company. Stay in touch with the demographics of your congregation.

Church socials also play an important role in helping maintain community and develop friendships. They provide avenues for people to hang out and meet other people, not just for marriage but also for companionship and mutual edification. For most of us, hanging out at the bar is not an option and internet dating is not for everyone. While the church is not supposed to be a dating service, it should remain a safe avenue that brings people together— sometimes romantically.

Lastly, I want to challenge you to review what you teach at your specialized fellowships. With the rise of feminism, women are twice as likely as men to file for divorce. Given that current trends in the world seem to eventually be mirrored in the church, there needs to be a deliberate effort to address the issues driving up the divorce rates. Women everywhere are bucking the conventions of gender roles and finding financial stability on their own while holding men to the same standards of fidelity women have been held to for generations. Feminism is on the rise, and if the church will not teach the balanced view, we risk creating a generation of women who will not have the resources needed to succeed in marriage the way God designed it.

IN CONCLUSION

I think I speak for every single woman out there when I say we would not be where we are today without the love and support of family, friends, and our church. If any thoughts

I shared in this section come off as offensive, please forgive me, as this was not my intention. I hope that reading through this gives you a different perspective on some issues that alienate single women, so we can all live together in godly harmony.

LIFE APPLICATION

1. What are the frequent flashpoints you encounter with the single women in your family?

2. What are the practical ways you can involve singles in your family activities?

3. Do you have a specialized fellowship in church that caters to your needs?

4. Which points resonated with you? Which ones do you have a different perspective on?

Wait—We're not Done Yet!

So what do we do now? What can we do while we wait, pray, and believe we will get married in God's good time?

The long and short of it is that the just shall live by faith. No matter what it is, we come back to the basic fact that we are Christians and must live like Christians as God commanded. Before you give up on me for being too "spiritual," allow me to explain what I mean by living by faith.

THE JUST SHALL LIVE...

Let's talk about what it means to live for a minute. Does this just mean breathing or a mundane day-to-day existence? Living things have certain characteristics that distinguish them from non-living things. I want to challenge you to live while you wait. Looking through the characteristics of living things, we find many pointers that show us what we need to do to truly live!

1. **Living things are made of cells.** Find a group of sisters to do life with. We are not made to live in isolation. If your current group of friends does not have your back, cannot laugh and cry with you, or do not lift you up when you are down—keep looking!

2. **Living things obtain and use energy.** Stop waiting for life to happen. What are you putting off for later that you can do now? John Maxwell says connecting with people requires energy![1] Spend your energy on being a blessing to people around you. Live out loud! Leave it all on the table! Bring energy to all you do!

3. **Living things grow and develop.** Use this time to grow in all aspects of your life. Take a Bible class, learn to bake, or pick up a new language. Whatever you do, don't stay stagnant—grow, develop!

4. **Living things reproduce.** You don't have to give birth naturally to be a mother. While you are waiting to get married and have your own children, mentor a child or young person. Get into the habit of pouring into the lives of the people you come in contact with.

5. **Living things respond to their environment.** Don't check out of life just because you are single. Be an active participant in your community and your church family.

---

1 Everyone Communicates, Few Connect – John Maxwell

6. **Living things adapt to their environment.** Adapt to life as a single person. Some of the most painful times for singles are around holidays and birthdays. Don't sulk during that time. Plan for the holidays and don't leave it to chance. When Valentine's Day comes, send a gift to one of your single friends and put a smile on their face. Stay with a roommate or move out on your own. Adapt to what works for you now that you are single.

> *The difference is the hope that lies ahead, that God will do what He promised to do.*

Living is much more than going through the daily motions with a "woe is me" attitude. What makes the difference is the hope that lies ahead, that God will do what He promised to do. What makes living a worthwhile alternative is faith!

...BY FAITH

We call Abraham "father" not because he got God's attention by living like a saint, but because God made something out of Abraham when he was a nobody. Isn't that what we've always read in Scripture, God saying to Abraham, "I set you up as father of many peoples"? Abraham was first named "father" and then became a father because he dared to trust God to do what only God could do: raise the dead to life, with a word make something out of nothing. When everything was hopeless, Abraham believed anyway, deciding to live not on the basis of what he saw he

*couldn't do but on what God said he would do. And
so he was made father of a multitude of peoples. God
himself said to him, "You're going to have a big family,
Abraham!"* (Romans 4:17–18 MSG)

An ordinary man achieved extraordinary results because
he didn't focus on what he couldn't do for himself. In like
manner, we can trust God to do what we are unable to do
for ourselves. Put your name in Abraham's place and trust
that God can and will put you in the right place at the right
time, and cause you to meet the person He prepared to be
your spouse.

_____ was first named "wife" and then
became a wife because she dared to trust God to
do what only God could do: raise the dead to life,
and with a word make something out of nothing.
When everything was hopeless, _____
believed anyway, deciding to live not on the basis
of what she saw she couldn't do, but on what God
said He would do. And so she was made a mother
of a multitude of peoples. God Himself said to her,
"You're going to have a big family, _____!"

We need faith to stay away from sexual sin. We need
faith to be free from destructive relationships. We need
faith to get married to a man God approves of. We need
faith to stay married. We will only be able to live by faith!
    Remember that faith grows as you study the Word
of God. Faith speaks the Word of God to circumstances
around it. Faith believes the promises God has spoken.

Faith acts on the instructions God has given. Faith hopes even in the face of the impossible.

As we wait, expect, and hope for marriage, know that every investment in your faith is a potential investment in your marriage.

TO WAIT OR NOT TO WAIT

If you have gotten this far in the book and still struggle with the decision to wait or not, let us spend time looking at other reasons we as women choose not to wait or wait with a bad attitude. What complicates the matter is that, at times, the right answer is to wait while other times, it is to fight! How do we know which one we should be doing in each circumstance? How do I know my continued singleness is not a result of inaction on my part rather than God working through a process? As Pastor John Miller[2] says—"Should I subscribe to the concept of 'Going until God says stop,' as opposed to "Not moving until God says go"?

Waiting is letting go of a compromising alternative because you trust there is something greater ahead of you

I have a near mortal fear of swallowing pills. When I was a child, it was quite the production getting me to take any medicine. I must confess, it's not much better now (I use gummy vitamins). After a while, I started refusing to take medication when I was ill on the premise I was trusting God for supernatural healing. Eventually, I had to be honest with myself.

2 Senior Pastor, Church on the Rock, Texarkana

The driver wasn't faith; it was fear. In so many cases, what we call waiting is nothing more than an excuse for inaction due to fear. Don't close yourself off from new relationships because of the pain from past ones. Don't hide behind activity to cover the pain and disappointment of failed relationships. Don't hide under the pretense of waiting!

For most of us, the issue is not waiting when we should be moving, or when we know the choice before us is wrong. Waiting is having the courage to let go of a compromising alternative because you trust there is something greater ahead of you. There are various reasons why we choose not to wait, and I will deal with a few of them here:

1. We forget that God has been faithful in the past

"But they soon forgot what he had done and did not wait for his plan to unfold" (Psalm 106:13)

The same God who saved you from sin gave you that job, and helped you with your studies is the same God who will bring your marriage to pass. Rebekah was only being a good neighbor when she connected to Isaac. Rachel wasn't looking for a groom when she went to the well and met Jacob. Ruth worked to provide for her mother-in-law, and in the process met Boaz and became the grandmother of David. Abigail was married to a fool named Naboth but only sought to do right by David. Remind yourself of what God has done for you, your friends, and even your enemies, then wait for His plan for you to unfold.

2. **Public opinion**

One thing I struggle with the most is public opinion. I wonder if people are looking at me and wondering why it is so difficult for me to get a man to marry me. The longer it takes, the more compelled I am to take matters into my own hands. The truth is, if we really didn't care about who we get married to, we could probably convince someone to tie the knot within a few months. After all, there are Christian women who are getting "married" to men who are already married elsewhere. Missionary dating and marriages still occur, with the woman deciding she would rather be married to an absentee man than remain single. Many of us, like Saul, feel compelled to offer the burnt offering because Samuel has not come to Gilgal at the time we thought he should. On the surface, it seems noble—it is better to marry than to burn. We testify to the church about what we have brought about with our hands while ignoring that he doesn't go to church anytime you are not with him. We excuse his abusive tendencies as having a bad day. We attribute his lack of focus to his being attacked by evil forces at work in his home.

But I encourage you today to wait! Ensure you are following God's plan for your life in marriage. Don't move ahead of God and compromise your standards because of

people around you—your parents, friends, or
relatives. Discover who you really are, not what
people expect you to be. Let your decisions be
based on what God says is best for you rather
than the opinions of others.

> *He waited seven days, the time set by*
> *Samuel; but Samuel did not come to Gilgal,*
> *and Saul's men began to scatter. So he said,*
> *"Bring me the burnt offering and the fel-*
> *lowship offerings." And Saul offered up the*
> *burnt offering. Just as he finished making*
> *the offering, Samuel arrived, and Saul went*
> *out to greet him. "What have you done?"*
> *asked Samuel. Saul replied, "When I saw*
> *that the men were scattering, and that you*
> *did not come at the set time, and that the*
> *Philistines were assembling at Mikmash, I*
> *thought, 'Now the Philistines will come down*
> *against me at Gilgal, and I have not sought*
> *the Lord's favor.' So I felt compelled to offer*
> *the burnt offering." "You have done a foolish*
> *thing," Samuel said. "You have not kept the*
> *command the Lord your God gave you; if you*
> *had, he would have established your king-*
> *dom over Israel for all time. But now your*
> *kingdom will not endure; the Lord has sought*
> *out a man after his own heart and appointed*
> *him ruler of his people, because you have*
> *not kept the Lord's command." (1 Samuel*
> *13:8–14)*

3. **It looks like it is taking too long**

I have been privileged to be chief bridesmaid
about ten times (I've lost count, I'm sorry).
One day a friend said about me, "She is like the
girl in the movie *27 Dresses*, i.e., the perennial
bridesmaid. While I know she meant no harm,
it made me wonder why I have to wait for so
many years when some women are on their
second marriages. It's much easier to wait when
we know when the end will come, but as thirty
rolls in, you are certain you will be married by
thirty-five. At fifty, it seems like a lost cause.
I take comfort in the promise it will come to
pass if I wait for it!

> *"For the revelation awaits an appointed time;*
> *it speaks of the end and will not prove false.*
> *Though it linger, wait for it; it will certainly*
> *come and will not delay"* (Habakkuk 2:3)

Commitment to Wait!

Taking the unpopular stance has never been
easy, but with God's help, this can be achieved.
The time of waiting is not when you should
throw up your hands and sit in despair. It is
a time of expectation that concentrates on the
joy set before you and prepares to enjoy the
fulfillment of the promise. I want to encourage
you to wait!

a) **Wait because there is a time for everything.**
Ecclesiastes 3:1–10 tells us there is a time for
everything and a season for every activity under
heaven. There is a time to love and a time to
hate! The word love used in this passage means
to have affection (sexually or otherwise) for
someone, i.e., love, like, friend. Understand
there is a season for love, and this is not the
same age for everyone. Your friends do not
determine your season for love, and you cannot
bring it about by force of your will.

b) **Wait because your times are in God's hands.**
In Psalms 31:5a, we understand, "Our times are
in His hands." One definition of the word "times"
is due season, and it's in God's capable hands.
Notice your due season is not in your hands, so
relax and let Him bring His perfect plan to pass
in your life.

c) **Wait because God knows your season of
love.** In Ezekiel 16:8, God was speaking about
Jerusalem being His bride and He said, "When
I passed by you again and looked upon you,
indeed your time was the time of love." The Holy
Spirit is with us and will guide us into all truth.
Rest assured that God's plans for you are only for
good and He will reveal your season to you by
His Spirit (1 Corinthians 2:6–14).

Debbie is single with a purpose

SINGLE AND ON FIRE

I have made up my mind to live life to the fullest. It shouldn't matter whether I get married or stay single, what should matter is I fulfill my purpose, and the pleasure of the Lord will prosper in my hands.[3] It's my time to discover who I really am, give of all that I have, and reach heights I have only dreamed of. It's my time to go on mission trips without having to make arrangements for hubby and kids. It's my opportunity to give sacrificially and train myself to put God first in my finances. It's my avenue to mentor and pour into the lives of my community and neighbors. It's my chance to volunteer and work diligently in the house of God. While I am waiting, I put God in the place of my husband and pour out my affection on Him. I spend time in His presence and strive to learn the true meaning of love—the agape that Christ displays for the church. Until that time comes, when He blesses me with the one He made me for, I will live every single day to please my audience of one!

Until that time comes, when He blesses me with the one He made me for, I will live every single day to please my audience of one!

I am single and on fire!

OUR GREAT CROWD OF WITNESSES

We have so many great examples of women in the Bible we can look up to for inspiration on how to live our lives.

---

3 Isaiah 53:10

We learn hospitality from Rebekah, who left her family to become the wife of Isaac. Rebekah did not treat Abraham's servant differently because he was not a prospective suitor. She went out of her way to help him without any hope of reward, and through her selflessness, she became the wife of one of the patriarchs of our faith.

We learn diligence from Rachel who worked as a shepherdess watching over her father's sheep. One ordinary day, she showed up at the well to water her sheep at the right time and met Jacob, her future husband.

We learn loyalty from Ruth, who stuck with her mother-in-law beyond the call of duty or the law. Even though there was no earthly way she could get another marriage, she chose the right thing over the "smart" thing and eventually became the grandmother of David.

We learn wisdom from Abigail, who was married to churlish Naboth but saved her household from destruction. Her wise choices led her to become the wife of the future king of Israel—David.

We learn humility from Esther, who became the queen of Persia because she listened to the right advice. This put her in a position to save the Jews from violence at the hand of Haman.

We learn leadership from Deborah, who was a prophetess, a wife, and a judge. She did not shirk the responsibility God placed in her hand. Instead, she arose "a mother in Israel."

We have so many examples of women cheering us on and telling us there are new heights to conquer and ground to cover. Don't let your marital status stop you from being the woman God has called you to be. Run the race—the world is waiting for you to shine!

> *Therefore, since we are surrounded by such a great cloud of witnesses, let us throw off everything that hinders and the sin that so easily entangles. And let us run with perseverance the race marked out for us, fixing our eyes on Jesus, the pioneer and perfecter of faith. For the joy set before him he endured the cross, scorning its shame, and sat down at the right hand of the throne of God. Consider him who endured such opposition from sinners, so that you will not grow weary and lose heart.* (Hebrews 12:1–3)

IN CONCLUSION

Your story is not done yet! We may not know the future, but we rest in the One who loves us and wants the best for you and me. Despite the obstacles and time it seems to be taking, God is still working on us as well as for us. His arm is not too short to reach us and turn things around. So when you feel down and out, reach down into the well of strength within you and remind yourself, I'm not done yet! You are more than a marital status. I leave you with these words from Paul:

> *And don't be wishing you were someplace else or with someone else. Where you are right now is God's place for you. Live and obey and love and believe right there. God, not your marital status, defines your*

life. Don't think I'm being harder on you than on the others. I give this same counsel in all the churches. (1 Corinthians 7:17 MSG)

LIFE APPLICATION

1. Which characteristics of living things are you doing well? Which ones do you need to do better?

2. What are the reasons you struggle to wait?

3. What does it mean to treat God as your spouse? Consider these two statements:

   ▸ I will treat God the way I will treat my spouse.

   ▸ I will treat my spouse the way I treat God.

   ▸ Which attitude needs adjustment?

4. What are the types of things you plan to do with your spouse that you can practice with God?

Acknowledgements

My editors—Paul Minor (Affordable Christian Editors), you took the rough draft and made it beautiful. Thank you for your words of encouragement! Pam Lagomarsino (Above the Pages)—for the proofreading! I am so glad I found you!

Michel Rohani—my book designer. Thank you for the work of art!

My cartoonist—Alastair Laird, you had the unique ability to take my scripts and translate what was in my mind to paper. You have a true gift!

Bishop Julius and Pastor Matilda Abiola—I bless God for your lives and the whole of Christ Life Ministries! Pastor Matilda—At a women's conference many years ago, you asked us to share our dreams and I spoke about my dream to minister to women. You asked the women to lay hands on me and always provided opportunities for me to minister to women at different conventions. You saw beyond the music minister to the speaker within me. You are a true mother in Israel!

Mama Adejumo—I look at you and wonder how you are able to accomplish all you do. When I grow up, I want to be like you! Thank you for honoring me and for the work you do building marriages around the world.

Church on the Rock Texarkana—I am blessed to call you my home church! Pastors John and Lanell Miller—thank you for giving to the Lord! You constantly show us that God saved us to be a blessing to other people! Pastors Mike and Sharon Ulmer—your humility amazes me. Pastor Nick and Delinah Birmingham—you know you are not just my worship pastor, you are now family. Kimi—my twin! I am always guaranteed a hug and a smile! Love you to bits. To the entire worship team—you guys rock!

My church family at Christ Life Bible Church in the Bronx! Thank you for everything!

Pastors Kayode and Odunola Tonade—who could ask for better pastors! Your large heart and godly example make me look forward to having my own home!

Sis Solafunmi Owoade—Big Sis, I finally finished it! I still hold fast to that message you taught—It was one ordinary day when David became king. It was one ordinary day when Joseph became prime minister. One ordinary day, God can turn your life around!

Sis Titi Olalekan—You prayed for me through this work! Thank you for honoring me with the responsibility of being godmother to your children!

Rev Elekima Ekine—you are a true spiritual father to me. From the day I told you about the dream of writing this book, you encouraged and pushed me till it came to fruition. You and Rev Mrs. have built a legacy in the lives of all us who grew up under your ministry in Christ Chapel International Churches Ibadan. I pray your seed will endure, your harvest will be plenty, and your joy will be full.

Pastors Debo and Funke Adedeji—your daughter wrote her first book! I appreciate you more than I can express! You opened your hearts to me and trusted me with your singles ministry at The Root of David Assembly (TRODA). I hope I have made you proud.

Coco Quarles—I thank God for connecting us not just as church family but as authors. I cannot forget the Sunday I sat in service asking God if I should stop writing this book. You came and sat by me and told me how I had been a blessing and I remember bawling my eyes out. God used you to encourage me when I was about to give up. I am so glad I was there for your book launch—the first of many! Watch out Texarkana—some Christian authors are on the loose!

Pastor Oyindamola Soderu—you were the first person to review the book who did not know me personally! I was not entirely sure if my family and friends were humoring me but your kind words were a breath of fresh air!

My band of sisters—Funmbi, Bukky, Chinny, Tayo, Cathy—you guys are the sum total of God's goodness to me. Whoever said that women do not encourage each other to greatness has not met you. Thanks for the help with editing and listening to all the angst whenever I got overwhelmed with finishing this book.

Funmbi—You were the first person I told about this book. Look what we did with it! I hope that now you finally have your friend back. I bless the day I met you.

Bukky—For the late nights, for connecting me with people I needed to, for being a listening ear! You have helped birth this book and I am grateful to have you in my corner! Look where God brought us from!

Chinny—My precious friend! Thank you for putting your editor extraordinaire skills to work on this book. I love that we think so alike—though I maintain you are a little crazier than I am! It takes great skill to challenge me and calm me down at the same time!

Tayo—Your insight amazes me! You look at an issue and just have a different perspective than the usual. I have enjoyed running things by you and learning from your wealth of wisdom.

Cathy—You have been a constant source of encouragement to me. Everyone needs a friend like you to cheer them on to greatness.

James Balogun—my friend cum brother. Thank you for continuing to push me to finish this book.

Enny—My "firstborn"! My baby is all grown up now! I marvel at the woman you have become. Thank you for all your help with the branding.

My family—Mama! I smile when I remember you calling and saying—I want to read my daughter's book! You are my greatest cheerleader and you have taught me more than you would imagine.

Bros Kay—My brother of few words. You said to me—"I have read the book. It is very well written. I believe it will be a bestseller. It addresses a topic that is not well focused on. It will definitely be a blessing to many. Not only singles" You do not know how those words have encouraged me. I can only say thank you for believing in me. Love you big Bro!

Browales—There are no words to express the depth of gratitude and respect I have for you. God has endowed you with so much wisdom and you live your faith with integrity. You know you are going to mentor my husband right?

Bjay—You are such a blessing to me! Thank you for all your encouragement and feedback. It's comforting to know I can always count on your support!

Olumide—Our very own celebrity! Thank you for the gentle nudges, the artistic direction, the push for excellence. God has so much in store for you my brother as you bring the sound of worship to the nations.

Tokunbo—My precious sister! In spite of your extremely busy schedule, you read every single word and gave me great feedback. What did I do to deserve you? You teach me every day that being a Proverbs 31 woman is not a pipe dream. Thank you for being the hand of God to me!

Itunu—You keep reminding me that I have been dethroned as the youngest Iyun. Thank you for always being there and being one of my main cheerleaders!

My nieces and nephews—Tiseyi, Semilore, Damilola, Damito, Tomisin, Ayanfe, Darasimi. Aunty loves you! It's been fun watching you guys grow up! Tiseyi and Tomisin—for all the hugs and calls and mother's day gifts, thank you! You help fill my love tank and this keeps me grounded!

My Texarkana Family—The Awuahs, Fomusos, Onipes, Mbonus, Ezihes, Antos, Majoros, Emechebes, Martins. You have made Texarkana a home for me! Thanks for praying for me as I was writing this manuscript!

Uche—thanks for prettying me up so I could look good in my photographs! I appreciate you, sis!

I have so many people to thank that I am certain I have inadvertently missed someone. So this is me saying—For all you have done, I pray God's blessing on you and all that are associated with you. Thank you! Thank you!

And to my Father—I have been listening to a Travis Greene song over the past few days and it expresses my heart so perfectly. It took me four years to eventually write the book You laid in my heart but "You waited for me, just for me! Where would I be if You left me, God?"

Whom have I in heaven but You! There is nothing on earth I desire besides You! You are my strength and my song, my glory and the lifter of my head, my help in times of trouble, my maker, my friend, my king, my lover, my husband. May all I do, all I am, all I have ever be to give You glory. May my life be a sweet scent of worship rising to You! Let my life o God praise You!

About the Author

Rotimi holds a Doctorate in Theology and is a John Maxwell Certified Speaker and Coach. Her writings have been featured in various magazines. She is a single woman in her late thirties who is passionate about God, women, and marriage or the lack of it. She will often be found with her nose in a book (actually her Kindle), running through an airport to catch a flight or singing on the worship team in her church.

Rotimi is the organizer of Deborahs Connect; an avenue for women to network and grow together in matters of faith, family, and work. She lives in Texarkana, Texas.

Connect with Rotimi at
www.rotimiiyun.com
Facebook: Rotimi Iyun, Author
Instagram: rotimiiyun
Twitter: rotimiiyun
Email: Timi@rotimiiyun.com

DEBORAHS
C O N N E C T

ABOUT DEBORAHS CONNECT

Deborahs Connect is a faith-based organization for women who want it all—a relationship with God, a wonderful family, and a great career. We believe that with God at the forefront and the support of a family, we can attain heights only imagined—without losing one or the other. Like Deborah, we stand as mothers in Israel—looking beyond our personal situations and making a difference in our environments.

We aim to help women become the best version of themselves through

- Online teachings and articles on faith, family, and work

- Workshops and specialized seminars

- Books and resources

  "Now Deborah, a prophetess, the wife of Lapidoth, was judging Israel at that time" (Judges 4:4 NKJV).

For more information, visit www.deborahsconnect.com or send an email to connect@deborahsconnect.com

Made in the USA
Coppell, TX
08 January 2022

71236975R00142